Alvon L. Fong
871 Orange Street
Yuba City, California 95991

facts for freemasons

By the Same Author:

1933*   *Lafayette, Citizen and Mason of Two Countries*

1935*   *The History of Organized Masonic Rosicrucianism*

1938‡   *The Eastern Star: The Evolution from a Rite to an Order*

1940*   *Negro Masonry in the United States*

1944*   *History of Knight Templary in New Jersey*

1945*   *Thumb-Nail Sketches of Medieval Knighthoods*

1952*   *Masonic Organizations and Allied Orders and Degrees*

1958*   *Masonic Rosicrucian Societies*

1960*   *The Royal Order of Scotland*

1960†   *Our Colored Brethren*

1963   *The Order of the Red Cross of Constantine*

1965   *The Story of the Scottish Rite*

1970   *General Lafayette, A Genealogy*

1970   *Loud and Clear: Story of the Liberty Bell*
        (co-author: Ronald E. Heaton)

1970*   *History of the Scottish Rite in New Jersey*

*Out of print
‡Revised 1976
†Revised 1970

facts for freemasons

A STOREHOUSE OF MASONIC KNOWLEDGE IN QUESTION AND ANSWER FORM

Compiled by

HAROLD V. B. VOORHIS, 33⁰

Fellow and Past Master,
American Lodge of Research, F. &A.M.
New York, N.Y.

Revised and Enlarged Edition

MACOY PUBLISHING AND MASONIC SUPPLY CO., INC.
RICHMOND, VIRGINIA

PUBLISHER'S FOREWORD

HAROLD VAN BUREN VOORHIS is a man of many interests and talents, and he has given 58 years of his 84 to Freemasonry since he became a Master Mason on June 11, 1920 in Mystic Brotherhood Lodge No. 21, of Red Bank, N.J., as historian, researcher, author, mentor and presiding officer in 34 of the 80 Masonic bodies in which he holds membership. He has received 8 special Masonic Medals and 5 Grand Crosses, a record for Masonic honors given to one man. Fifty-year buttons have come to him from the Grand Lodge, Chapter, Council, Commandery and Scottish Rite. In 1950 he was made a 33^0 Scottish Rite Mason. In recent years he has relinquished the duties as leader of many of the Masonic bodies but he remains Supreme Magus of the Masonic Societas Rosicruciana in Civitatibus Foederatis, which office he has held for over 26 years, the longest on record.

Mr. Voorhis holds the unequaled distinction of being Grand Representative of the Grand Lodge, F. &A.M., Grand Chapter, R.A.M., Grand Council, R.&S.M., and Grand Commandery, K.T., all of North Carolina, in similar bodies in New Jersey. He is the Grand Representative in the U.S. of four Masonic bodies in England, Ireland, France and Switzerland.

He is the author of 26 books and more than 100 brochures and articles; he compiled three genealogies, including one on General Lafayette. His research articles on "Rob Morris: An Almost Forgotten Man of Freemasonry" and on Robert Macoy have provided data never before known.

More than 70 non-Masonic organizations claim Harold Van Buren Voorhis as a member, including The Holland Society of New York which presented him the President's Medal in 1971.

Mr. Voorhis was a pioneer in radio. He became interested in "wireless" in 1908 when only 14 years old and lectured and explained by illustrations the United Wireless system, a combinaton of the DeForrest and Fessenden systems, to the Physics Class in Red Bank, N.J. High School. He gained publicity as a radio "ham" in the N.Y. *Herald Tribune* as well as in *Short Wave News*, London, England, and before 1925 had made 60 receiving sets for others. He became a member of The American Radio Relay League in 1922 and Patron of MARN, an international Masonic Radio Society. In 1976, he was made a Fellow of the Radio Club of America.

The Van Voorhees Association lists Mr. Voorhis as one of the founders. He has made an extensive study of the Bible and many religions; he was interested in photography and stamps and pursued these hobbies over a period of years; he made a study of foods and nutrition and was quite a cook, but his profession was as a chemist. He served in World War I; attended Columbia University in New York City and became chemist for Bull and Roberts, Inc. of that city from which he retired in 1962. He has been a Vice President of Macoy Publishing & Masonic Supply Co., Inc. since 1946 and has given valuable assistance.

One of his idiosyncrasies—he always wears a *red* tie.

While Mr. Voorhis' talents have benefited many in many divergent interests, his most outstanding contribution has been to his fellowman through his love and service to Freemasonry. This company is indeed grateful for his revision of this new edition of *Facts for Freemasons*.

THE PUBLISHERS

AUTHOR'S FOREWORD

The works of many authors have been consulted in the preparation of this compilation. A work such as this can only be prepared by reference to the publications of others, but the bulk of the material is the result of original research which I have conducted over a period of many years. Much of the data have not previously been printed elsewhere. To those whose works have been consulted I extend my grateful acknowledgment and thanks.

I will welcome any letters which point out errors in dates or other historical discrepancies. On controversial points, probably agreement cannot exist, for interpretations are many and each must seek answers according to the light given him.

The book is arranged so that one may turn to the section which interests him most by referring to the Contents listing which follows this Foreword.

If I have disillusioned any reader of his concept that Freemasonry, as it is practised today, began in Biblical, or earlier time, I have not tried to rob unkindly. I simply call attention to the fact that while we revere the past, Freemasonry stands today on what it is NOW, for age means naught if not accompanied by improvement because of it and a resulting "good works." In this Freemasonry needs bow to no organization–fraternal or otherwise!

HAROLD VAN BUREN VOORHIS

May, 1951
Revised, January, 1977

CONTENTS

PART I

Forerunners of Freemasonry

1. Where did Masonry originate?

No one knows. It is believed to have had its roots beyond historical record and, like religion, to have evolved—possibly by way of the Egyptian Mysteries—down to modern times through various organizations. We do know that many of the symbols came from groups or organizations of medieval times.

2. From what groups, or organizations, are the symbols used in Freemasonry believed to have been derived?

The Roman Collegia of Artificers or Comacines, the Ancient Mysteries, the Cathedral Builders, the Rosicrucians, and the Stone, or Operative Masons.

3. Who were the Comacines?

Groups of operative craftsmen attached to Roman legions who traveled with the legions into the conquered provinces. Members of such guilds, or crafts, built churches, cathedrals, temples and other great structures. They were greatly in favor in medieval times and were recognized by the Popes and accorded special privileges and protection until the early part of the 14th century when Pope Benedict XII came to power. Gradually, these Comacine Masons lost the favor of the papal authorities and were suspected of being a secret society.

4. Who were the Ancient Mysteries?

There were several societies, religious in character, who taught morality by symbolism. The Druids was a secret order in England and France, or then, Gaul. Their ceremonies were symbolical and were divided into three orders.

1

5. What are the Mysteries of Mithras?

They were part of the Ancient Mysteries. Mithras was worshipped as the God of Light in Persia. Zoroaster is supposed to have instituted these mysteries as an initiation into the principles of religion which had been founded among the ancient Persians.

6. Who were the Cathedral Builders?

Stone Masons who traveled throughout Europe building cathedrals. They were known as free-masons because they enjoyed the freedom of traveling about. The Reformation brought about a lessening of power in the Catholic Church and cathedral building diminished and with it the once powerful Cathedral Builders.

7. Who were the Rosicrucians?

Those, who, in the 17th and early part of the 18th centuries, claimed to belong to a secret society and to have knowledge giving them mystical and magical powers.

8. What were the principal objects of Rosicrucian search?

The universal solvent—The Philosopher's Stone, thereby striving to acquire the power of transmuting baser metals into gold, and of indefinitely prolonging human life.

9. What connection, if any, existed between the Freemasons and the Rosicrucians?

Both employed a large number of symbols in common.

10. From what particular country are our Masonic symbols derived?

"From Egypt, the land of the winged globe, the land of science and philosophy, peerless for stately tombs and temples, the land whose civilization was old before other nations since called to empire, had a name."

11. Who built the Great Pyramid of Gizeh, and for what purpose was it built?

Cheops (Khufu). One of its purposes, and perhaps the principal one, was to serve as an astronomical observatory.

12. What are the Seven Ancient Wonders of the World?

The Pyramids of Egypt. The largest pyramid, located at Giza (a short distance from Cairo), is that of the Pharoah Cheops (Khufu). It covers 13 acres and originally was 481 feet high. It was erected about 2680 B.C. The Egyptian pyramids are the only surviving ancient wonders of the world.

The Mausoleum at Halicarnassus. Erected *c.* 352 B.C. about a hundred miles south of modern Izmir, Turkey. A marble tomb of the Persian satrap of Asia Minor, Mausolus of Caria. Demolished by an earthquake in the 15th century. Its sculptors were the Greek Scopas and Praxiteles. Fragments are in the British Museum, London.

The Great Temple of Artemis (Diana) at Ephesus. Built about 550 B.C. Dedicated to the worship of Artemis, an earth goddess. Destroyed in 262 A.D. by invading Goths.

The Hanging Gardens of Babylon. A terraced flower and vegetable garden built by Nebuchadnezzar II, in the 6th Century B.C. Remains of its walls are located south of Bagdad.

The Colossus of Rhodes. A huge bronze statue of the sun god Helios, built overlooking the harbor of Rhodes about 285 B.C. Destroyed by an earthquake about 244 B.C.

The Olympian Zeus. An ivory and gold statue of the Greek God which was carved by Phidias between 437 and 425 B.C. for the temple at Olympia. Centuries later destroyed by the Goths or Vandals.

The Pharos (lighthouse) at Alexandria. Completed about 280 B.C. by Ptolemy II, Greek king of Egypt. Demolished by an earthquake in the 14th Century.

13. Where is the Temple of Karnak?

Luxor, on the old site of Thebes, on the eastern bank of the Nile River.

14. Of what especial interest is this Temple to Masons?

It is constructed with a rare unity of design, testifying to a cooperative system.

15. What was the design of a sphinx?

A monster having a lion's body, wings, and the head and bust of a woman.

16. From whom does Masonic tradition say the Egyptians received Operative Masonry?

From their great progenitor, Mizriam, the grandson of Noah.

17. How many workmen were required to build the Pyramid at Gizeh?

Herodotus says it took 300,000 men thirty years.

18. Who were the Copts?

Egyptians of the native race descended from the Hamites who have preserved, from their ancestors to the present day, much information relating to Masonic symbolism.

19. What Egyptian King enforced the worship of the "solar disk" upon his subjects?

Amen-hotep.

20. What is the Egyptian Naos?

The ark of the Egyptian gods. A chest, or structure, with more height than depth, and, therefore, unlike the Israelitish Ark of the Covenant. The winged figures embraced the lower part of the Naos, while the cherubims of the Ark of Jehovah were placed on the lid.

21. Why were sphinxes erected in front of temples and places of initiation?

To denote that all sacred truth is enfolded in enigmatical fables and allegories.

22. Who was Hermes Trismegistus?

It is questionable if such a person actually existed. The accepted belief is that he was a celebrated Egyptian legislator, supposed to have lived in the "Year of the World 2670" as "Hermes, Thrice Great." From the arts attributed to him, or his time, we are supposed to have the basis of various Hermetic Rites and Hermetic Masonic degrees.

23. How did the ancient Egyptians picture Osiris?

As the All-Seeing Eye.

24. What is the Temple of On?

The Temple of the Sun in the city of On in lower Egypt, between the Nile and the Red Sea. The Greeks know the city as Heliopolis.

25. Why were mythological tales invented?

An abstruse treatise is difficult to remember. A mythological tale can be retained in the memory with ease and communicated to another, together with the key for its interpretation.

26. Why did the ancient priests make use of hieroglyphics?

It was considered unlawful to commit scientific knowledge to writing, therefore, when it became necessary to preserve such knowledge, hieroglyphics were used.

27. Why did all ancient buildings contain a system of Masons' marks?

To show by whom the work was done.

28. What is the probable age of the Circles of Stonehenge in England which represent the sun and the twelve signs of the zodiac?

It was oriented as a sun-temple about 1650 B.C.

29. From whom did the Greeks borrow much of their architecture, art and learning?

The Egyptians.

30. The most celebrated ancient oracle "neither spoke nor kept silence but revealed by signs." Where was it?

It was the Oracle of the King at Delphi, Greece.

31. Who discovered the "Forty-seventh Proposition of Euclid"?

Pythagoras, said Anderson in his 1738 edition of the *Constitutions.*

32. What is the Tetragrammaton?

A Greek word signifying "four letters." It is a name given by the Talmudists when referring to God, or Jehovah.

33. Why do Masons revere Pythagoras?

He was one of the most remarkable and able of Greek philosophers. He was a pupil of Zoroaster and adopted many of his virtues. He established schools in Crotona which were of a secret order. The symbolism in his Grecian Mysteries of three degrees bears analogy to the symbols of the Masonic three degrees and some claim that esoteric Masonic doctrines are derived from Pythagorean Schools, founded upon temperance and love of work. Pythagoras paid great attention to the Science and Numbers whose mysteries are found in the *Kabbalah* and in all of the occult Masonic studies.

34. Masonic history contains many references to the "Nine Muses." Who were they?

Calliope, Clio, Erato, Euterpe, Melpomene, Polyhymnia, Terpsichore, Thalia, and Urania.

35. Who were the Cyclops?

A fabled race of giants having but one eye in the middle of the forehead. They were said to have assisted in Vulcan's workshops.

36. What was the phoenix, and of what was it the emblem?

A miraculous bird, an embodiment of the sun god, and according to fable, lived 500 years, to be consumed in fire and to rise in youthful freshness from its own ashes. Therefore, an emblem of immortality.

37. Who made use of the phoenix for his seal?

Aumont, Grand Master of the Templars after de Molay.

38. To what Roman deity does Tubal Cain correspond?

Vulcan.

39. Why is the Vesica Piscis of such great importance as a symbol?

The method of delineating or plotting; it was one of the great secrets of church architecture.

40. Who were the Dionysian Artificers?

An organization of builders in Asia Minor about 1000 B.C. During the Crusades, they journeyed into Europe and merged with other traveling masons.

41. Who was Callimachus?

A noted Greek architect and artist, and the originator of the Corinthian Column.

42. What is considered the finest example of Corinthian architecture?

The Pantheon at Rome, Italy, is considered the finest of the ancient type of Corinthian architecture.

43. Of what value to Freemasons is a knowledge of modern archaeology?

Masonic research students have learned much about the ancient Mysteries, Mithraism, the Collegia, and beginnings of the guild system and of European architecture.

44. Who were the Culdees?

A fraternity of priests, constituting an irregular monastic order, existing in Scotland, and in smaller numbers in Ireland and Wales, from the 9th or 10th to the 14th or 15th century.

45. What were the "guilds"?

Workers in the same line of endeavor, who organized their own guild, or fraternity, and had their own regulations, admitted members on oath, meted out punishments for violations, imposed fines, accepted apprentices and trained them.

46. Did they have a national organization?

No. The guilds were local, but their methods of work and training were about the same everywhere in England and in Europe and a guildman could move from one country to another in expectation of becoming a member of a similar guild.

47. Who were the Masons in the Middle Ages?

The word "mason" denoted a builder and was connected with architectural construction at first, then only to such as worked in stone, bricks, and tiles. Later, those connected with such construction, such as engineers and helpers, were so-called.

48. How long were apprentices required to serve before they were thought to know enough to become a Fellow of the Craft?

Seven years. At the end of that period the apprentice might make his "Master's Piece" and submit it to the Master and Wardens of his craft for their acceptance or refusal.

50. Why are the guilds of particular interest in Freemasonry?

From them came the Operative lodges of masons and then Freemasonry as we know it today.

51. What is the legend regarding Jabal and the Swastika?

God taught Jabal to build a house of stone with four rooms in the form of a swastika. By this plan, when the winds were very strong from one quarter, the inmates could move to the opposite quarter and so obtain safety and comfort.

52. How did Jabal conceal the secret of his building?

By covering the whole of the stonework with wood, within and without. When a great gale blew down the houses of wood, Jabal's building stood firm. Then said the people, "How is this, for our houses are wrecked, but this building of wood is not wrecked?"

53. What three classes of guilds existed in England?

Religious guilds under patronage of the Church of Rome; Merchant guilds exemplified in the Livery Companies of London; Craft guilds, similar to the present day trade unions.

54. Who were the Operative Masons?

Among the different groups of builders was one which confined itself to architecture. The craftsmen in this guild, or fraternity, were called "Freemasons" because they were free to move from city to city, or country to country.

55. What great discovery did the Operative Masons make in the 12th century which has had great influence on the world's architecture?

Construction of Gothic architecture which called for men who could master arts and sciences not known to others at the time, men as great in mind as in skill. These *Operative Masons* produced an architecture which had never been equalled, except by the Greeks, and the Gothic has never since been surpassed.

9

56. Who were the "Four Crowned Martyrs"?

Four Operative Masons who were put to death during the reign of the Roman Emperor Diocletian for refusing to assist in the construction of pagan temples. They were adopted as Patron Saints of Operative Masonry by the stone-masons of Germany. *The Regius MS.* of the *Constitutions of Freemasonry* relates the legend and this manuscript was titled "Ars Quatuor Coronatorum" from which the famous literary lodge, Quatuor Coronati No. 2076 of London, took its name.

57. What is Tectonic Art?

The science of building temples and other important buildings and working in stone in accordance with the "ancient usages and established customs" of the Operative Masons.

58. When did Operative lodges cease to be active as such?

Between 1710 and 1730 when the Speculative Masons gained control, and the formation of the first Grand Lodge in 1717.

59. What is the difference between Operative and Speculative Masons?

Operative Masons were actually stone-masons engaged in actual construction work up through the 17th century. The Speculative Masons were non-working stone-masons, corresponding to what we would term "honorary members" who were taken into the Operative lodges.

60. How early were Speculative Masons taken into Operative lodges?

The earliest minute entry found anywhere, so far, is of a non-Operative being present in a lodge on June 8, 1600, when John Boswell, a landlord of Auchinleck, Scotland, is listed as being present in a Lodge of Edinburgh.

61. When do we first hear of a Grand Lodge of Speculative Masons?

In 1717 when a group of Speculative Masons of four London lodges met in that city and organized the premier Grand Lodge of Freemasonry in the world for the purpose of governing the lodges in that city.

62. Why is modern Freemasonry called "Speculative"?

To distinguish it as a system of speculative, or contemplative, science from an operative art.

63. What is Speculative Masonry?

It is another name for Freemasonry in its modern acceptance. It is the scientific application and the religious consecration of the rules and principles, the language, the implements, and materials of Operative Masonry; it is a system of ethics.

64. One of the many theories of the origin of Freemasonry gives much credit to Francis Bacon, a Rosicrucian. Has this any foundation?

No. Masonic students, after subjection to every literary and critical test of *The Old Charges*, refute this. Bacon published his *The New Atlantis* in 1627 in which he dealt with a fabled island in the Pacific Ocean, and the culture and customs of its inhabitants.

65. Where was Lemuria?

A tract of land supposed to have formerly extended from Africa and Madagascar to India; one of the submerged continents.

66. Who were the Xerophagists?

After the ban against Freemasonry on April 28, 1748, by the Roman Catholic Pope, many Catholic Masons continued to meet under that name. *Xerophagist* comes from two Greek words meaning "those who live without drinking." All such bodies introduced a pledge of total abstinence in their by-laws.

11

67. Who was Flavius Josephus?

A Jewish writer of the 1st Century who wrote *A History of the Jewish War* in Syro-Chaldaic; later he translated it into Greek. Some Masonic degrees were drawn from the works of Josephus.

PART II

Biblical References and King Solomon's Temple

1. What are some of the emblems of Freemasonry mentioned in the Bible?

Lambskin (Peter 1:19; Prov. 27:26); Pot of Incense (II Chron. 4:22; Rev. 8:3; Ex. 38:3; Heb. 9:4); All-Seeing Eye (Prov. 15:3; Ps. 11:4; Ps. 33:18); Anchor and Ark (Heb. 6:19; Heb. 11:7); Scythe (Job 14:2; Is. 38:10); Sword Pointing to Naked Heart (St. Luke 2:35); Acacia (Ez. 27:19).

2. From what portion of the Bible does the penitential hymn of King Solomon, "Remember now thy Creator in the days of thy youth," come?

Ecclesiastes 12:1.

3. What is the Eucharist?

The sacrament of the Lord's Supper; also the consecrated elements.

4. What is the meaning of the name of the first man?

ADAM is derived from the Hebrew aDaMaH, meaning "the ground."

5. How long was Noah and his family in the Ark?

One solar year of 365 days.

6. How many windows were in the Ark?

The Bible says one.

7. How many times did Noah send out the birds from the Ark, and what birds were they?

Three. First, a raven and a dove; second, a dove; and third, a dove.

8. Why did the Jewish people abstain from pronouncing the name JEHOVAH?

Possibly to conceal it from the surrounding heathen nations and thus not have the name desecrated by having it applied to idols.

9. Who was Enoch?

The eldest son of Cain.

10. What three sects occupied Judea at the time of Christ?

The Pharisees, the Sadducees, and the Essenes.

11. Who said, "Am I my brother's keeper?"

Cain.

12. Who are some Biblical characters used in Masonic degrees?

Moses, Aaron, Joshua, Eleazar, Solomon, Adoniram, Abda, Hiram, King of Tyre, Cyrus, Artaxerxes, Zerubbabel.

13. Whose rod, when dropped to the ground, became a snake, and when picked up became a rod again?

Aaron's rod. (Exodus 7:10) At another time it blossomed, budded and bore fruit in a day. (Numb. 17:8)

14. Upon what is the super-structure of Freemasonry built?

The Hiramic Legend, which is a retelling of the belief in the immortality of the soul.

15. What was its source?

The Old Testament. (See I Kings and II Chronicles)

16. Who built the Ark of the Covenant and what was kept in it?

Moses built it at God's command and the two tables of stone on which were the Ten Commandments were kept in it. The Ark was first kept in the most sacred part of the Tabernacle, and later removed to King Solomon's Temple.

17. What name is given Acacia in the Bible?

Shittim wood. (Exodus 25:10)

18. How long were the Israelites kept captive in Egypt?

430 years.

19. Whom did God command Moses to say had sent him into Egypt to deliver the children of Israel?

I AM THAT I AM. (Exodus 3:14-15)

20. Did Moses ever enter the Promised Land?

No. The Lord called him up from the plains of Moab to Mount Nebo where Moses could see the Promised Land, but he was not to pass over into it. Moses died at the age of 120 years.

21. Who was Solomon?

The son of David and Bath-Sheba. He was born about 997 B.C., became King 977 B.C. and died about 937 B.C.

22. What does the name Solomon mean?

Peaceful. King David gave his son this name in anticipation of the peaceful years which he believed were to follow.

23. Where do we get the expression "the wisdom of Solomon"?

When Solomon became King at the early age of about 20, God came to him in a dream and asked of Solomon what he desired. His request was an understanding heart that he might judge and rule wisely.

24. How many years did Solomon reign over Israel?

40 years.

25. What command of his father, King David, did Solomon carry out?

The building of the Temple. King David was not permitted to build it because he had been a man of war.

26. Where was the Temple built?

On Mount Moriah. David had purchased the land from Ornan, the Jebusite. In II Sam. 24:18-25 it is stated that he paid 50 shekels; in I Chron. 21:18-27, the price is stated as 600 shekels of gold.

27. What was this site called?

The threshing floor of Ornan.

28. How old was Solomon when the Temple was started?

About 25 years of age.

29. How long did it take to build the Temple?

Seven and one half years.

30. Where in the Bible do we read of the story of the building?

I Kings, beginning with chapter 5 and also in II Chronicles, beginning with chapter 2.

31. Who was Hiram of Tyre?

A great friend of King David, who, when King Solomon asked for cedar trees, readily agreed to furnish them for the Temple.

32. Who was Hiram Abif?

A widow's son of the tribe of Naphtali, a man from Tyre, and a worker in brass, who came to aid King Solomon in the building.

33. Who was Aholiab, and what did he do?

He was a master craftsman who was appointed to help construct the tabernacle in the wilderness and the Ark of the Covenant.

34. Whom did Solomon appoint as his Captain of the Guards?

Azariah.

35. What part did Adoniram play in the building of the Temple?

He was chief receiver of tribute under David, Solomon, and Solomon's son, Rehoboam.

36. Did the Pillars in the Porch of King Solomon's Temple originate in the Masonic allegory?

No. They are represented in many monuments of much greater age.

37. What is the meaning of the alleged fact that in the building of the Temple there was not heard the sound of axe, hammer or any tool of iron?

That character is builded in silence; that discordant sounds should not be permitted to disturb the harmony of the Lodge.

38. What is the symbolic meaning of King Solomon's Temple?

This was the most perfect edifice ever erected and therefore symbolized perfect development of mind and character.

39. What was the Middle Chamber of the Temple?

There were three stories of side chambers built around the Temple on three sides. The Middle Chamber was the middle story and served for the accommodations of the priests. Their sacred vessels and vestments were kept there.

40. How did Solomon reach the middle and third chambers of the Temple?

By winding stairs.

41. What is the Masonic symbolic meaning of the Middle Chamber?

The abiding place of truth, reached by the winding stairs.

42. What is the Biblical meaning of the "hewn stone"?

A symbol of evil and falsehood.

43. What is the Masonic symbolism of "hewn stone"?

This came from the Operative Masons and the perfect ashlar, or hewn stone, is the symbol of man's improved and perfected nature.

44. Where was Joppa?

The seaport of Jerusalem from which it was 40 miles distant. The King of Tyre sent ships to Joppa laden with timber and marble to be forwarded overland to King Solomon for the construction of the Temple. Joppa is now called Jaffa.

45. Where were the "clay-grounds" from which the sacred vessels of the Temple were cast?

Between Succoth and Zeredathah.

46. When the Temple was completed what special ceremonies did Solomon hold?

He directed that the Ark of the Covenant be brought from the King's house, where his father, David, had kept it and that it be deposited in the Sanctum Sanctorum.

47. What was in the Ark when it was brought to the dedication of the Temple?

"There was nothing in the Ark save the two tables of stone, which Moses put therein at Horeb." (II Chron. 5:10)

The New American Bible. The first Roman Catholic Bible translated directly into English from the original biblical Hebrew, Aramaic, and Greek. Modern in style and language and is rapidly replacing *The Douay Bible* in the U.S.

The Jerusalem Bible. A modern translation of the Bible for the French-speaking world done by French Catholic scholars in Jerusalem (1947-1956).

74. What is the Jewish version of the Scriptures in English called?

The Holy Scriptures According to the Masoretic Text, published in 1916. Also,

New Jewish Version scheduled for publication in completed form in the 1970s. This English-language Bible is in contemporary style, in some cases greatly altering familiar phrases. *The Pentateuch* (first 5 books) has been published.

75. Has the V.S.L. always been a part of the Furniture of the Lodge?

The latest evidence is that it was. The statement concerning William Preston's motion in the Grand Lodge of England in 1760, that the Bible be made one of the Great Lights, is without foundation as Preston was not made a Mason until March 21, 1763.

76. Why is the Book of the Law open in the Lodge?

Because it is the Great Light of Freemasonry and to close it would be to intercept the rays of divine light which emanate from it. When spread open it indicates that the Lodge is not in darkness. A closed, or sealed, book indicates that its contents are secret. Hence, the V.S.L. is opened to teach that its contents are to be studied and that it is to be the "rule and guide of our conduct."

77. Do Masonic lodges in the U.S. open the Bible at the same passages?

No. In each degree there are appropriate passages. In some jurisdictions the Bible is opened at random, but since the publication of Webb's *Monitor*, the custom in the United States has been fairly uniform and is as follows: 1st Degree: Psalms 133; 2nd Degree: Amos 7:3; 3rd Degree, Ecclesiastes 12.

78. At what passages do some lodges in England open the Bible?

1st Degree: Ruth 4:7; 2nd Degree: Judges 12:6; 3rd Degree: I Kings 7:13-14.

79. Should all Masons be obligated on the Christian Bible?

No. Masonry is universal and men of every creed are eligible for membership so long as they accept the Fatherhood of God and the Brotherhood of Man. Therefore, the candidate should be obligated on the Book of the Sacred Law which he accepts as such since his obligation is a solemn and a binding one.

80. What are the Sacred Books for the Mohammedan, the Hindu, the Parsee, the Brahmin, the Jew?

Mohammedan—*The Koran;* Hindu—*The Shastras;* Parsee—*Zoroastrian Code* or *Zend-Avesta,* consisting of the *Avesta* (Bible) and its *Zend* (interpretation); Brahmin—*The Vedas;* - Jew—*The Old Testament* only may be preferred.

81. In lodges which have members of different races and creeds, what would be the proper procedure?

It is customary to have several holy books upon the altar so that the candidate may choose that which is to him the most sacred.

82. How many Bibles are used in lodges in Ireland?

Three; one on the altar in the center of the room and one on each of the Wardens' pedestals.

83. Why did the Grand Orient of France, in 1877, remove the Bible from the altar and delete prayers from the ritual?

To emphasize the Masonic principles of universality and its adherence to the doctrine of the separation of Church from the State. The Grand Lodge of France and the National Grand Lodge of France retain the Bible on their altars.

84. What action did this bring forth?

Nearly all of the Grand Lodges, especially English-speaking ones, never recognized the Grand Orient thereafter.

85. Is this still the case?

Yes.

86. What Biblical character was embalmed and "put in a coffin in Egypt" when he died?

Joseph. (Gen. 50:26)

87. What was the Vulgate?

A Latin version of the Scriptures made by Jerome at the close of the 4th century. So called from its common use in the Latin Church.

PART III

Beginnings of Freemasonry in England

1.   From what preceding organization is Speculative Freemasonry directly descended?

From the Operative Masons of England.

2. When were "permanent lodges" organized?

The earliest minutes extant of "permanent" lodges are those of just prior to the 1600's [Aitcheson's Haven, 1598 and Edinburgh (Mary's Chapel) No. 1, 1599] although existence of even earlier ones may be surmised. They were Operative lodges, some of which became Speculative. These are the types of lodges which formed a Grand Lodge in London in 1717 and from which each and every regular lodge or Grand Lodge in the world today traces its history.

3. Did these "permanent lodges" keep records or documents?

Yes, as in the case noted above, many lodges had minutes and other documents.

4. What are The Old Charges?

Declarations of authority based on inherent rights from operation since time immemorial, usually by royal authority. In the Middle Ages all groups, such as guilds, schools, churches, etc. were required to have a written charter or similar official instrument in writing testifying to their legality. These documents were granted by the king, the borough, or the bishop. The Freemasons claimed (and they were not disputed by the authorities) that during the reign of King Athelstan he had given his official approval and granted the Fraternity a *royal* charter. A *royal* charter outranked all others. When the first permanent lodge was set up, the Freemasons did not petition for a new charter, but submitted a claim by means of a document to the royal charter. This claim became a most famous document and was reproduced hundreds of times in the future and came to be called *The Old Charges.*

5. Were these reproductions of The Old Charges identical?

No. There were many copies and versions, the oldest being the *Regius MS.* which was written about 1390 A.D.

6. What did The Old Charges contain?

They began by stating that the art of Freemasonry was very ancient as well as honorable, and continued to be true to its royal charter; they ended by giving the rules and regulations under which lodge members were governed.

7. How did the ritual originate or evolve?

Originally, it was not composed as a ritual, nor was it a series of ceremonies. It was the perpetuation of activities, practices and usages of the daily work and customs of Operative Masons. It was not called a ritual, but the "work."

8. What is the earliest date that Masons have had a separate and organized self-governing society?

H.L. Haywood, one of America's outstanding authors, thinks that the date may be as early as 1541, which is the earliest period of Protestantism. His assumption is based on the fact that there are written records proving a continuing existence of Masonry in Aberdeen from 1264 and that doubtless this Scottish Lodge has an unbroken line of descent from the 13th century.

9. Who is credited with being the "father of modern Speculative Freemasonry"?

Dr. John T. Desaguliers, elected third Grand Master in 1719. However, the first and second Grand Masters, Anthony Sayer and George Payne, respectively, did little more than act as chairman and Dr. Desaguliers was in actuality head of the new Grand Lodge for four years. He served three terms as Deputy Grand Master.

10. Who was Elias Ashmole?

The author of *Ashmole's Diary*. This volume contains two references to Freemasonry. Ashmole was made a Mason in the Lodge at Warrington in Lancashire, England, October 16, 1646. He is supposed to have been a Rosicrucian and one of the first Speculative Masons.

11. Where was the first Speculative Grand Lodge?

On St. John the Baptist's Day, June 24, 1717, four London lodges met and organized the premier Grand Lodge of Freemasonry.

12. Did this Grand Lodge control all Masonry in England?

Not at first, but later it assumed control. As time went on most of the English lodges became affiliated with it.

13. Were there the same three degrees in the lodges of 1717 as at present?

No. At first there seems to have been a single degree and a Master's part. Within about ten years there emerged three degrees or ceremonies of advancement and, finally, a fourth part which became the Royal Arch Degree.

14. Did the Grand Lodge finally control all Masonry in the entire British Isles?

No. Grand Lodges were established in Scotland and in Ireland a few years later. The Operative bodies in these countries were the foundation for their information as they were in England.

15. Is the present Grand Lodge of England the only Grand Lodge ever established in that country?

No. There have been several others; all but one finally ceased working for various reasons.

16. Which was the one which did not cease working?

The "Antient" or "Atholl" Grand Lodge.

17. How and when did this Grand Lodge come into being?

Irish Masons residing in England formed this rival Grand Lodge in London in 1751. They called the older Grand Lodge the "Moderns."

18. How is it easy to distinguish the "Antients" from the "Moderns"?

The "Antients" were the newer Grand Lodge and the "Moderns" were the older one.

19. When did these two Grand Lodges combine into the present "United Grand Lodge of England"?

In 1813.

20. What was the main difference of opinion between the rival Grand Lodges?

The "Antients" accused the "Moderns" of neglecting the ceremony of installation—a ceremony equivalent to the R.A. degree.

21. What Declaration was made at the union?

That

"(2) pure Ancient Craft Masonry consists of three degrees and no more, viz.: those of the Entered Apprentice, the Fellowcraft and the Master Mason, including the Supreme Order of the Holy Royal Arch. But this article is not intended to prevent any lodge or chapter from holding a meeting in any of the degrees of the Order of Chivalry, according to the constitutions of the said Orders."

[This last sentence is no longer in the book of *Constitutions* of the U.G.L. of England.]

22. Does the United Grand Lodge of England control all Masonic lodges now in England?

Technically, the answer is no. However, those lodges which it does not control are ambulatory lodges. These are Irish Military lodges. One of these, Leswarree, No. 646, warranted in the 8th King's Royal Irish Hussars, was consecrated at Aldershot, England, in 1932.

23. What was the name of the first English Grand Master?

Anthony Sayer, Esq.

24. Who was the Grand Master of the "Antient," or rival, Grand Lodge of England after which this body was later named?

The 4th Duke of Atholl, who served two terms: 1775-1781 and 1791-1813, when the union took place. He was also Grand Master of the Grand Lodge of Scotland, 1778-1779.

25. At the time of the union of the two Grand Lodges of England, in 1813, what was an oddity concerning the Grand Master of each?

They were blood brothers: Edward, Duke of Kent and Augustus Frederick, Duke of Sussex.

26. Who became Grand Master after the union in 1813?

The Duke of Sussex.

27. How many of the four original lodges, which constituted the premier Grand Lodge of England, are still in existence?

Apple Tree Lodge (now Fortitude and Old Cumberland No. 12); Rummer and Grapes Lodge (now Royal Somerset House and Inverness No. 4); and Goose and Gridiron Lodge (now The Lodge of Antiquity No. 2).

28. What three dates are important in early Freemasonry in England?

1717 relates to the time of the formation of the first Grand Lodge. 1751, a second Grand Lodge was formed as a result of a disagreement. 1813, the two divisions again united in harmony of purpose and formed the United Grand Lodge.

29. Who called the assembly of Masons in York, England, in 926 A.D.?

King Athelstan. This date was used by Anderson in his *Constitutions*, but Gould said 932 was more likely the proper date.

30. There are constant references to the founding of a Grand Lodge at York, England, in the year 926. Has this been substantiated?

No, it is purely a tradition.

31. What style of architecture was intimately connected with Masonry in the Middle Ages?

Gothic, or the pointed arch.

32. What celebrated Operative Mason erected St. Paul's Cathedral in London?

Sir Christopher Wren.

33. Who were the "Scald Miserables"?

The name given to persons in 1741 who formed a mock procession in derision of Freemasonry.

34. What society was organized in England, about 1723, in opposition to the Freemasons?

The Gormogons. No Freemason could be made a member until he had renounced the Masonic Order. The Gormogons claimed they were descended from an ancient Chinese society.

35. What English Queen is said to have sent an armed force to York with intent to break up the Grand Lodge?

Queen Elizabeth.

36. Who was James Anderson?

He compiled the first *Book of Constitutions* which was published in 1723.

37. Who was Laurence Dermott?

Publisher of the *Ahiman Rezon* and Grand Secretary and Deputy Grand Master of the "Antient" Grand Lodge. He was a link between the "Antients" and Ireland because he received the Royal Arch there.

PART IV

Beginnings of Freemasonry in America

1. American Freemasonry came from what country?

England. Both Grand Lodges of England had Provincial Grand Masters in the Colonies; also, the Grand Lodges of Scotland and Ireland either had Provincial Grand Masters, or started lodges, in America.

2. What is the earliest mention of Freemasonry in America?

There are five unauthenticated "legends" dated 1606, 1658, 1670, 1715, and 1720. (1) A rock with the date September 6, 1606 and some markings resembling a S.&C. was found at Annapolis Basin, Nova Scotia, in 1827. (2) Fifteen Jewish families came to Newport, Rhode Island, from Holland, in 1658. Mordecai Campannall and others of the group were claimed to have been Masons. (3) The Apostle, Eliot, was supposed to have sent a box containing Masonic emblems from England in 1670, to be forwarded to Charleston, South Carolina. (4) There is mention of a letter written in 1715 by John Moore, a King's Collector, who had come from England in 1680, in which he had written that the winter had been a long and dull one with little pleasure except "a few evenings spent in festivity with my Masonic brethren." (5) There is a story of a lodge held in King's Chapel, Boston, Massachusetts, in 1720.

3. What were the four earliest Masonic lodges in the Colonies?

Tun Tavern, Philadelphia, Pennsylvania; First Lodge, Boston, Massachusetts; Solomon's, Savannah, Georgia; Solomon's, Charleston, South Carolina.

4. Approximately, what years were these lodges started?

1730, 1733, 1734, and 1735, respectively.

5.   What is the first regular and *duly constituted* lodge in America?

St. John's Lodge, Boston, Massachusetts, July 30, 1733.

6. Why isn't Tun Tavern Lodge in Philadelphia considered the first since it was started about 1730?

Lodges were working in Massachusetts, Pennsylvania and elsewhere as early as 1730 by prescriptive right, but legal authority to constitute lodges according to the English regulations adopted in 1722 was given June 5, 1730. However, there is no record extant showing that such authority was used until July 30, 1733.

7. Who was the first recorded Mason to become a permanent resident of America?

John Skene, whose name is 27th on the roll of members of Aberdeen Lodge No. 1, Scotland. He came to America in October, 1682, and settled in Burlington, New Jersey. He became Deputy Governor of New Jersey and died while in office in 1690.

8.   Who was the first native born American to become a Freemason?

Jonathan Belcher, Governor of Massachusetts and New Jersey, who was made a Mason in 1704 while on a visit to England.

9. Which is the oldest Grand Lodge in the United States?

The Massachusetts Grand Lodge, A.F.& A.M. (1777) but this is not without question due to some subsequent happenings. The present G.L. of Mass. really dates from 1792. Virginia, in 1778, actually formed the first Grand Lodge as they exist today.

10. When were independent Grand Lodges established in the United States?

Following the Revolutionary War.

11. Between what years were the first thirteen Grand Lodges formed?

1777 and 1796.

12. Where did lodges meet in Colonial times?

In private residences, taverns and inns.

13. What effect did the rivalry between the two Grand Lodges of England have upon American Masonry?

The Grand Lodge of Antients became very popular in the Colonies. Provincial Grand Lodges emanating from this Grand Lodge were set up in the following: New York, Pennsylvania, Virginia and South Carolina, where they worked as "Ancient York Lodges."

14. Was there a union of the two rival groups in the various states?

Yes; the two rival Grand Lodges working in South Carolina were the last to combine (1817).

15. What Grand Lodge in the U.S. still adheres to the work of the Ancients?

Pennsylvania.

16. What was the attitude of the Colonial lodges toward the American Revolution?

Members of the Ancient lodges evinced a greater disposition to espouse the cause of the Colonies, while the Moderns inclined to side with the Crown.

17. Who was the first Provincial Grand Master in America?

Colonel Daniel Coxe (1673-1739), who served in the office June 24, 1730 to June 24, 1732.

18. Who was Henry Price?

Another famous Provincial Grand Master of New England who was born in England in 1697 and died in Massachusetts in 1780. He was appointed to the office in April of 1733 while in London. The document of appointment is generally believed to have been dated the 30th, although the late Melvin M. Johnson, P.G.M., has shown that it most likely was the 13th of the month. Price served until 1737. Later, he served two more terms: 1754 to 1755 and 1767 to 1768.

19. What part did the Masons play in the famous "Boston Tea Party"?

Most of the participants in the history-making raid were Masons and the planning of the raid had its inception in a Masonic lodge room.

20. Who did more to establish Freemasonry in America during Colonial times than any other of his time?

Benjamin Franklin.

21. What was the first Masonic book printed in America, and by whom?

Franklin reprinted Anderson's *Constitutions* in 1734. This is commonly known as the "Franklin Reprint." Seventeen copies of the original edition are in existence. It is the rarest American Masonic book.

22. What Revolutionary General from Massachusetts was killed at the Battle of Bunker Hill?

General Joseph Warren, Scottish Provincial Grand Master and leader of the "Antients" in Massachusetts.

23. A famous Frenchman presided at the cornerstone laying of the Battle of Bunker Hill Monument. Who was it?

Lafayette.

24. What distinguished Massachusetts Mason has been commemorated in poetry and story because of a famous ride?

Paul Revere, who later became the first Master of The Rising States Lodge (1774) and Grand Master, 1794-1797.

25. What black man lived during Revolutionary times in Massachusetts whose name has been perpetuated in black Masonry in the United States?

Prince Hall, first black man to have been made a Freemason in America and first Grand Master in the first black Grand Lodge, later named Prince Hall Grand Lodge.

26. Were there many Masons among the officers of the Revolutionary Army?

Yes. Washington, 14 Major-Generals, 44 Brigadier-Generals (all but one), and many others of lesser rank.

27. Who was the foremost naval officer of the Revolutionary period who was also a Mason?

John Paul Jones, father of the American Navy.

28. What Frenchman, a Mason, became an officer of the Continental Army and served with Washington?

Lafayette.

29. Where was Lafayette made a Freemason?

There are several unauthenticated accounts of his entrance into Freemasonry, but none has been proven. There are, however, many accounts of his presence at Masonic meetings.

30. Where was Washington made a Mason?

In "The Lodge at Fredericksburg," in Virginia, initiated on November 4, 1752, his entrance fee having been two pounds three shillings. He was "pass'd fellow Craft" March 3, 1753, and raised as Master Mason, August 4, 1753.

31. Was Washington ever Master of his Lodge?

No, but he became a charter member and the first Master of Alexandria Lodge No. 22, Virginia, where he served two terms, April 28, 1788 to December 27, 1789.

32. Has any President of the United States ever been Master of his Lodge while President?

Yes, but only Washington, who was Master at the time he was inaugurated President of the United States on April 30, 1789.

33. What is the name of Alexandria Lodge No. 22, of Virginia, now?

Alexandria-Washington Lodge No. 22—so named in 1805 after Washington's death.

34. Was Washington ever a Grand Master?

No. The Convention which resulted in the formation of the Grand Lodge of Virginia nominated him, but he declined. He was also named as prospective Grand Master of a General Grand Lodge proposed about the same time.

35. Who introduced a resolution at a National Masonic Congress in Washington, D.C. to organize a National Grand Lodge?

Henry Clay.

36. How many signers of the Declaration of Independence were Masons?

Benjamin Franklin (Pa.), John Hancock (Mass.), Joseph Hewes (N.C.), William Hooper (N.C.), Robert Treat Payne (Mass.), Richard Stockton (N.J.), George Walton (Ga.), William Whipple (N.H.) are definitely proved to have been Freemasons.

There are 24 others credited as having been Freemasons, but their records are questionable. There are 24 known to have been non-Masons.

The original document signed in the afternoon of July 4, 1776 (now lost) showed two names: John Hancock, the President of the Continental Congress and Charles Thompson, Secretary (not a member but the attestant). On July 19th the Continental Congress ordered an engraved copy of the Declaration which was finally signed by the 56 delegates. This document is now in the National Archives Building in Washington, D.C. *(See Coil's Masonic Encyclopedia, page 624)*

37. How many Presidents have been Freemasons?

Up to the present time (1978), 16. They are:

> George Washington (1732-1799), raised in the lodge at Fredericksburg, Va., Aug. 4, 1753.
>
> James Madison (1751-1836), lodge unknown.
>
> James Monroe (1758-1831), E.A. in Williamsburg No. 6, Va., Nov. 9, 1775. He was only 17, but the lawful age had not been fixed as 21. There is some evidence that he was later raised in an Army lodge.
>
> Andrew Jackson (1767-1845). While there are no records to date to show where he was raised, it is well known that he was a Freemason from records of his many visitations. He was Grand Master of the G.L. of Tennessee from 1822-23.

James K. Polk (1795-1849), Columbia Lodge
No. 31, Columbia, Tenn., Sept. 4, 1820.

James Buchanan (1791-1868), Lodge No. 43,
Lancaster,Pa., Jan. 24, 1817.

Andrew Johnson (1808-1875), Greeneville
Lodge No. 119 (now No. 3),
Greeneville, Tenn., May 5, 1851.

James A. Garfield (1831-1881), Columbus
Lodge No. 30, Columbus, Ohio, Nov.
22, 1864.

William McKinley (1843-1901), Hiram
Lodge No: 21, Winchester, Va., May 3,
1865.

Theodore Roosevelt (1858-1919), Matinecock
Lodge No. 806, Oyster Bay, N.Y., April
24, 1901.

William Howard Taft (1867-1930) was made
a Mason "at sight" at an Occasional
Lodge called for that specific purpose,
Feb. 18, 1909, Cincinnati, Ohio.

Warren G. Harding (1865-1923), Marion
Lodge No. 70, Marion, Ohio, Aug. 27,
1920.

Franklin Delano Roosevelt (1882-1945),
Holland Lodge No. 8, New York City,
Nov. 28, 1911.

Harry S. Truman (1884-1972), Belton Lodge
No. 450, Belton, Mo., March 18, 1909.
Grand Master of the G.L. of Missouri,
1940. Thirty-third degree, A.& A.S.R.,
Oct. 19, 1945.

Lyndon B. Johnson (1908-1973), Johnson
City Lodge No. 561, Texas, E.A. Oct.
30, 1937.

Gerald R. Ford, Jr. (1913-   ), Malta
Lodge No. 465, Grand Rapids, Mich.,
May 18, 1951.

38. How many Vice-Presidents have been Freemasons?

Seventeen.

We have had 41 Vice-Presidents (1978), 13 of whom went on to become President. Of these 13, Truman, Johnson and Ford were Freemasons. Of the other 28 who did not become President, 14 have been proved to have been Freemasons, as follows:

4—George Clinton, Warren Lodge No. 17, N.Y.

5—Elbridge Gerry, Philanthropic Lodge, Mass.

6—Daniel D. Tompkins, Hiram Lodge No. 72, N.Y.

9—Richard M. Johnson, Hiram Lodge No. 4, Ky.

11—George M. Dallas, Franklin Lodge No. 134, Pa.

13—William R.D. King, Phoenix Lodge No. 8, N.C.

14—John C. Breckinridge, Des Moines Lodge No. 41 (now No. 1), Iowa.

17—Schuyler Colfax, St. Joseph Lodge No. 45, Ind.

23—Adlai E. Stevenson, Metamore Lodge No. 82, Ill.

24—Garrett A. Hobart, Falls City Lodge No. 82, N.J.

26—Charles W. Fairbanks, Oriental Lodge No. 500, Ind.

28—Thomas R. Marshall, Columbia City Lodge No. 189, Ind.

33—Henry A. Wallace, Capitol Lodge No. 110, Iowa.

38—Hubert H. Humphrey, Cataract Lodge No. 2, Minn.

39. What has been done to perpetuate the name of Washington in Freemasonry?

Many lodges (as well as cities and schools) are named for him; the Washington Masonic Memorial in Alexandria, Virginia; the George Washington Degree (20th) in the Scottish Rite of the Northern Jurisdiction.

40. Who was the most famous of Washington's biographers?

The Reverend Mason Locke Weems, a member of Lodge No. 50, in Virginia, who wrote a *Life of Washington* which went into about seventy editions. It is largely a few facts "buried beneath a preponderance of pietistic drivel and grandiloquent panegyrics."

41. What is the one thing that is most remembered from Weems' book?

The "Cherry Tree" story which appeared only after a few editions had been printed. Weems was the *sole* authority for this tale of George and his hatchet.

42. Who, in more recent times, has written a more historical treatment of the life of Washington?

Rupert Hughes. In 1976, Allen E. Roberts gave us his *G. Washington: Master Mason*, an honest recording of the Masonic story of Washington. Of the many books written about George Washington, this is one of the few which approaches the man from a human interest standpoint.

43. What famous contemporary of Washington named his son George Washington?

Lafayette.

44. Two of Washington's Masonic aprons have been preserved through the years. Who presented these to him?

One was made by French nuns and presented at Mt. Vernon, Virginia, by Watson and Cassoul, his French agents, both of whom were Masons. It is owned by Alexandria-Washington Lodge No. 22, Virginia. The other apron was made by Lafayette's wife and presented to Washington at the same place. This apron was owned by the Washington Benevolent Society, Philadelphia, but now belongs to the Grand Lodge of Pennsylvania and may be seen in the Lodge Museum and Library at Philadelphia.

45. Where and when was Washington sworn in as President of the United States?

On the Sub-Treasury steps, Wall Street, New York City, the Capitol at that time, on April 30, 1789. He was Master of his lodge at the time.

46. What Bible was used for this ceremony?

A Bible was borrowed from St. John's Lodge No. 1, N.Y.C. General Jacob Morton was Marshall of the Day and Morton was also Master of St. John's Lodge which met nearby. The Bible is still in possession of St. John's Lodge.

47. Who administered the oath of office?

Chancellor of State Robert R. Livingston, also Grand Master of the Grand Lodge of New York at the time.

48. When did Washington lay the cornerstone of the Capitol Building in Washington, D.C.?

On September 18, 1793, in the *south*-east corner. Washington wore the apron which Lafayette had presented to him. The trowel which he used is still in the possession of Alexandria-Washington Lodge No. 22.

49. What is the "Golden Urn"?

An urn which holds a lock of Washington's hair. It was presented to the Grand Lodge of Massachusetts in 1800 by Washington's widow.

50. What famous Masonic Revolutionary General became a traitor?

Benedict Arnold. He was a member of Hiram Lodge No. 1, Connecticut, with which he affiliated April 10, 1765. There is no record of the lodge in which he was raised.

51. What modern Masonic degree depicts some of the events connected with Washington and Arnold?

The 20th degree of the Scottish Rite as conferred in the Northern Jurisdiction of the U.S.A.

52. What was probably the first organized religious opposition to Freemasonry in the U.S.A.?

A convention of Baptist churches held at Milton, Saratoga County, New York, on September 12th and 13th, 1827.

53. What was the "Morgan Affair"?

On September 12, 1826, William Morgan, living in Batavia, New York, was abducted from a Canandaigua, N.Y., jail and conveyed to Fort Niagara, N.Y. No trace of him has ever been found after September 19th of that year. His name, as author, is attached to an exposé of Freemasonry printed by David C. Miller (who had received the E.A. degree only), proprietor of the "Republican Advocate," a month prior to the abduction. It is claimed that Morgan was murdered by Freemasons, but no evidence has proved that he was even killed. No record has been found that he was a member of a lodge, but he was made a Royal Arch Mason in Western Star Chapter, No. 35, Le Roy (now Batavia), New York, May 31, 1825.

54. What was the result of this incident?

An anti-Masonic political party was formed in 1831 and William Wirt of Maryland was the Presidential nominee. He carried the state of Vermont only in the election.

55. Why was Wirt opposed to Freemasonry?

He was not. He was a Fellowcraft in Jerusalem Lodge No. 54, Richmond, Va. (1808 *Proc.*) and defended the Order in a speech before the Convention which nominated him.

56. By 1830 the anti-Masonic excitement had gained such momentum that 124 of the 983 newspapers of the United States had been established on the principle of opposition to Freemasonry. Of these 124, 99 were in what two states?

New York had 46 and Pennsylvania had 53.

57. In Batavia, New York, there is a monument erected to the memory of William Morgan, fifty-six years after the "Affair." Who was accused of murdering Morgan on one of the inscriptions on the monument?

The Freemasons.

58. What is the American system in Masonry?

Five rites: Ancient Craft (or Symbolic Masonry); Royal Arch (or Capitular Masonry); Council (or Cryptic Masonry); Templar (or Chivalric Masonry); Scottish Rite.

59. Who made an attempt to have a uniform ritual adopted in the United States?

Rob Morris of Kentucky organized a group called "The Conservators" to attempt this, but uniformity in the United States has never been attained.

60. Who were the Mound Builders?

A pre-historic race of North American people who wrought physical works that offer evidence that the highest civilization yet indicated anywhere upon the earth flourished on this continent while India, Egypt and Babylon were in their infancy. All their remains show a definite geometrical plan, involving squares, oblongs, and circles.

61. What conclusions may we draw from the measurements of the earth-works of the American Mound Builders?

That their dimensions correlate with those of King Solomon's Temple and the Great Pyramid, and express the same mathematical ratios. All are embodiments of the solar system.

62. Were some of the early American Indians Freemasons?

There is no evidence to prove that they were. They did use a symbolical language as have peoples of all ages.

63. We have often heard or read of stories whereby a Freemason was saved because he gave a Masonic sign to an attacking Indian. Are these fairy-tales?

Not necessarily so. Symbolism is a universal language and could very well have been the cause for leniency in some cases.

64. Who was the Mohawk Indian who did save a Revolutionary Captain's life because he was a Mason?

Joseph Brant who was initiated in 1776 in London. During the Revolutionary War he was in command of some Indian troops fighting for the British. Captain McKinsty of the Colonial Army had been captured and was about to be tortured by the Indians when Brant discovered the Captain to be a Mason, rescued him and eventually had McKinsty returned unharmed to a Colonial outpost.

65. What famous Southerner's library was saved by a Union officer during the siege of Little Rock?

Albert Pike's library was saved because Grand Master Benton, of Iowa, a Union officer, posted guards around Pike's home with instructions that the home and contents were not to be razed.

PART V

Early Books, Monitors, Constitutions
and Authors

1. Where is the first mention of Masonry?

In a poem called *The Halliwell Manuscript*, named after James Orchard Halliwell who discovered it in the British Museum and published it in 1840 and again in 1844. It is also known as the *Regius Manuscript*. The original poem is dated by antiquaries at 1390.

2. What is the first printed mention of Freemasonry in America?

The word "freemason" appeared in the *Boston News Letter* of January 5, 1718.

3. What is the oldest Masonic document in existence in the United States?

The ledger for 1731 of St. John's Lodge of Philadelphia.

4. What was the first Masonic book printed in America?

Franklin reprinted Anderson's *Constitutions* in Philadelphia in 1734.

5. Who published the first Masonic monitor?

William Preston, London, England, in 1772. The title was *Illustrations of Masonry* and eighteen editions were printed over a period of years.

6. Who published the first Masonic monitor in the United States?

Thomas Smith Webb published his *Freemason's Monitor* in 1797 at Albany, N.Y. This was reprinted in many editions.

7. For what is Jeremy L. Cross best known?

For his *True Masonic Chart, or Hieroglyphic Monitor*, first issued in New England in 1819 and ran through seventeen editions. This was practically the Webb *Monitor* with illustrations added.

8. Who is the author of the definition of Freemasonry as "a beautiful system of morality, veiled in allegory and illustrated by symbols"?

Samuel Hemming, an expert ritualist and first Senior Grand Warden of the United Grand Lodge of England.

9. Name other authors of monitors which were published in America.

Atwood, Chapman, Chase, Davis, Drummond, Howe, Lightfoot, Macoy, Mead, Morris, Sickels, Simons, Stewart, Tannehill, and Taylor.

10. Who wrote *A Defence of Masonry*?

Martin Clare, a golden-tongued orator and zealous advocate of the new Grand Lodge system in England in the middle of the 18th century.

11. What caused him to write it?

The appearance of *Masonry Dissected*, 1730, an exposé of Freemasonry, by Samuel Pritchard. It was reprinted in *A Defence of Masonry*.

12. Did this stop the writing of exposés?

No, there have been dozens of them since.

13. Who wrote the epilogue entitled "House of Solomon"?

Sir Francis Bacon.

14. What did the "House of Solomon" describe?

The island of Bensalem (Sons of Peace) and on it a structure called the House of Solomon which housed a fraternity of philosophers devoted to the acquisition of knowledge.

15. In the early 19th century catechisms there are references to the "yellow jacket and a blue pair of breeches" as the clothing of a Master. What is one explanation of this?

The yellow jacket is the compasses and the blue breeches, the steel points.

16. What Russian novelist gave a description of the initiation of a Mason?

Count Tolstoi in *War and Peace.*

17. Name famous Scottish and English authors whose works contain Masonic references.

Robert Burns in "Farewell to Tarbolton Lodge"; Rudyard Kipling in *The Man Who Would be King, Debits and Credits, The Palace, Kim, The Mother Lodge, L'Envoi, In the Interest of the Brethren;* Sir Arthur Conan Doyle in *The Red Headed League.*

18. Name famous early American authors whose works contain Masonic references.

Lew Wallace in *The Prince of India;* Edgar Allan Poe in *The Cask of Amontillado.*

19. Who were early German authors whose works contain Masonic references?

Goethe in *Wilhelm Meister* and a poem, "A Mason's Ways"; Gottfried Lessing in *Ernst and Falk* and *Nathan the Wise.*

20. Who was the most famous English Masonic historian?

Robert Freke Gould.

21. Who was the most famous 19th century American Masonic historian?

Albert G. Mackey.

22. What was the first Masonic magazine published in the United States?

"The Freemason's Magazine and General Miscellany," in 1811.

23. Who wrote the most famous *Constitutions of Freemasonry*?

Rev. James Anderson, in London, in 1722, but though approved in that year, the book was not published until 1723 and hence is known as the *Constitutions of 1723*. A second edition was published in 1738.

24. Are Anderson's *Constitutions* followed by all Grand Lodges of Freemasonry?

No, each Grand Lodge has a Constitution of its own and they vary greatly in detail. However, fundamentally, they all agree.

25. Is the Franklin Reprint of 1734 *Constitutions* rare?

It is the rarest Masonic book printed in America. Only seventeen copies of the original are known to exist.

26. By what general name are the forerunners of the printed *Constitutions of Freemasonry* known?

The Old Charges.

27. In what form did these "Ancient Charges" exist?

In manuscripts or manuscript rolls.

28. What is the heading of Charge I in the 1723 printed *Book of Constitutions?*

"Concerning God and Religion."

29. How many such manuscripts are known?

Approximately 100.

30. Are these Old Charges alike?

No, the minor and major differences have caused Masonic scholars to reduce them to classes in trying to trace them down through the years.

31. What is the *Polychronicon*?

A Latin chronicle written by Ralph Higden in 1350, and later translated into English. It was largely drawn upon by the compilers of the Old Charges of Masonry.

32. What writers compiled Masonic encyclopedias?

Kenning, (actually compiled by Rev. A.F.A. Woodford, but published by his friend Kenning and is known as *Kenning's Cyclopedia*,) Mackey, McKenzie, Macoy, Waite, Coil.

33. Who compiled the first Lexicon of Freemasonry in the United States?

Albert G. Mackey of South Carolina, in 1845. He drew heavily from the Lenning-Mossdorf Lexicon published in three volumes in Germany, circa 1822.

34. Was there an earlier Lexicon?

Yes, Johann Gaedicke, a bookseller in Berlin and a devout Freemason, published a number of Masonic books, among them a lexicon in 1818.

35. What types of Masonic books were most popular in the late 18th and early 19th centuries?

Pocket Companions, Masonic Charts, Masonic Monitors, Masonic Registers, Masonic Almanacs, Engraved Lists of Lodges.

36.   Why was the publication of *The Use and Abuse of Freemasonry,* **in 1783, by Captain George Smith, of importance?**

Prior to that time only monitors or handbooks had been sanctioned by the Grand Lodge, in addition to the Constitutions. Grand Lodge frowned on the publication of Masonic books of a general nature and refused permission for the printing of Smith's book. He defied the censorship and published his book anyway which had a large circulation. It is not an important book in content, but from then on Freemasons were free to write books.

37.   Who wrote what is considered the first comprehensive and more, or less, standard Masonic history?

Robert Freke Gould of England. He has been called the Thucydides of Masonic history.

38.   Who was Thucydides?

A Greek historian born 471 B.C.

39.   What is the first line of the funeral dirge used by Freemasons in the Master Mason degree?

"Solemn strikes the funeral chime."

40.   What is the last line of this dirge?

"Take us to Thy Lodge on High."

41.   Who wrote this funeral dirge?

David Vinton, one of the early "traveling Masonic Lecturers," born January 6, 1774 at Medford, Massachusetts, and died at Shakertown, Kentucky, in July, 1833.

42.   When did the dirge first appear?

In the "Masonick Minstrel," published in Dedham, Massachusetts, 1816.

43. Are the words used today as originally written?

Yes, but only four of the eight stanzas are used.

44. To what music was this dirge set?

To *Pleyel's Hymn.*

45. Who was Pleyel?

Ignaz Joseph Pleyel was an Austrian, born in 1757 and died in 1831. He manufactured pianos and wrote church music which was very popular in his day.

46. David Vinton, who wrote the funeral dirge was also the author of an androgynous degree. What is the name of that degree?

The Heroines of Jericho.

47. What is the title of the book in which first appeared the word "freemason"?

A Booke in English metre, of the great Merchant man called Dives Pragmaticus, published in 1563. In the same year there also appeared a book by John Shute entitled *The First and Chief Grounds ... of Architecture.* It was written for builders, or freemasons, and is a treatise on the Five Orders. From an operative sense, it is "Masonic," but the word "Freemason" does not appear. Nine books were published at intervals between 1598 and 1708. In 1709, "The Tatler" in its issue of June 9th, made reference to "Free-Masons," and in the same periodical for May 2, 1710, appears: "One . . . would think that they had some secret intimation of each other like the Freemasons." There is one publication listed for the year 1717, one for 1719, six for 1721, and nine for 1722.

48. In what do we find the earliest probable use of the word "accepted"?

The Harleian Constitution of 1670 states that "no person shall be accepted a Mason unless he shall have a Lodge of five Freemasons....no person shall be accepted a Freemason but such as are of able body, honest parentage..."

49. What famous Scottish Rite Mason of the 19th century wrote his hundreds of manuscripts by hand?

Albert Pike; he used a quill pen.

50. There have been thousands of books written about Freemasonry. Some were written by women; who were they?

Mrs. Blake, of London, wrote *The Realities of Freemasonry*, 1879; *Occult Theocrasy*, by Lady Queenborough (Edith Starr Miller), was printed in France, in English, 1931. *Secret Societies and Subversive Movements*, by Nesta H. Webster, was printed in London in 1924.

51. Under what name is the book of laws of a Grand Lodge known in this country?

The Digest, or The Code.

PART VI

Masonic Customs and Regulations

1. Is Freemasonry a secret society?

Only as to its modes of recognition and passwords. There is no secrecy as to its organization, principles, or purposes.

2. Is Freemasonry a religion?

No, but it is religious. It does not require a particular church affiliation and only asks a candidate that he believe in a Supreme Being and some form of future existence.

3. Is Freemasonry a benefit society?

It offers no form of insurance, but it need yield to none in works of charity.

4. Is Freemasonry a political organization?

No, but it does impress upon its members that they have civic duties to perform through channels of expression outside its lodges.

5. What is the connecting bond between all lodges of the world, aside from ritual?

Lawful authority as no lodge can exist and work without this recognition.

6. What are the three main attributes necessary for a man to become a Freemason today?

To be of lawful age (21 in the U.S.); have a good character; to have means of support. In recent years, some Grand Lodges have lowered the age to 18.

7. There are three ways in which a man may become a member of a lodge. What are they?

By being elected and initiated; by affiliation; by being elected an honorary member or fellow.

8. Should Masons conduct "membership drives"?

No. Masonry does not seek members. Each prospective member knocks at the door of the lodge hall of his own free will.

9. How then can we flourish and prosper and spread our teachings?

By conducting ourselves in such a manner as to make other men, especially young men, want to join us in our work. We must take the teachings of the Craft into our daily lives and set an example for the uninitiated.

10. Is it permissible to withdraw a petition for membership once it has been presented before the lodge in the United States?

In some jurisdictions the petition cannot be withdrawn. In others it may be withdrawn if the recommenders request it. However, if the Committee reports, the petition cannot be withdrawn.

11. What is the difference between a ballot and a vote?

The ballot is one method of voting; the vote is the act. Other methods of voting are by showing of hands or by acclamation.

12. What should be done with the ballots as soon as the result is announced?

The presiding officer should return the balls and cubes to the drawer of the box, thus leaving the ballot box proper clear. The ballot box should be presented to and returned from the Master only in a clear condition.

13. A number of Grand Lodges have changed their laws so that black balls are no longer used for balloting. What are used?

Black cubes.

14. What prompted this change?

To prevent errors resulting from poor sight. The round balls are white and the cubes are black so that one may know by the sense of touch how he is balloting.

15. What officer of the lodge may be excused from voting by the consent of himself, the Master, and the brethren present?

The Tiler.

16. What officer in a Masonic body uses the Baton?

The Marshal.

17. What officer of the lodge is armed with a weapon?

The Tiler—a sword.

18. What officer of the lodge cannot participate in the "work" of the lodge, or enter into any of the business without special permission of the Master?

The Tiler, who must be relieved in order to enter the lodge.

19. Can a Masonic lodge exist and be legally constituted, but not recognized?

Yes. The terms "clandestine," "regularity" and "recognition" have always been used in confusion among Masonic bodies. Many Grand Officers simply take their *Constitutions* (which often label the three the same) as a basis for saying all lodges not recognized by them are "irregular" and/or "clandestine" when actually this may not be true.

20. When did the word "clandestine" first appear?

In the 1784 *Book of Constitutions*, by Noorthhouck, in a foot-note.

21. In this country can a Grand Lodge have jurisdiction over a lodge outside of the continental United States?

Yes. Massachusetts has jurisdiction over lodges in the Canal Zone and China; Washington has jurisdiction over lodges in Alaska; and California has jurisdiction over lodges in the Hawaiian Islands.

22. Do all Masonic jurisdictions allow dual or plural membership?

No, some allow one only. Others allow membership in two similar Masonic bodies. And some allow plural, or membership in an unlimited number of lodges. The last is true in many foreign countries.

23. Are the rituals in the Grand Lodges in the British Isles uniform?

No, there are variations between lodges, just as there are in the United States between Grand Jurisdictions.

24. In order that a Freemason may visit a lodge other than his own, what is required?

To have a paid up receipt for dues and to be able to pass an examination which will "prove himself a Mason," or be vouched for by an admitted brother present.

25. Is there an official examination in use for the purpose of examining a visitor?

No, each Grand Jurisdiction uses such method as seems best for the purpose. Some have an official catechism; others ask pertinent questions, but all require the "Master's Word."

26. Who can overrule the objection of a lodge member to having a visiting Mason seated?

No one while the objecting brother is present.

27. May an unfavorable ballot be discussed?

No. The secrecy of the ballot is inviolate and no brother is permitted to ask how another will, or has, balloted.

28. Why are there divergencies of the ritual?

Due to the formation of several Grand Lodges. Attempts were made twice at Baltimore, Maryland (1843 and 1847) to agree on uniform work. Such attempts failed as did the plan for a National Grand Lodge in the United States. Consequently, each Grand Lodge maintains practically uniform work within its own jurisdiction.

29. What formerly governed the time of opening of a lodge?

They were opened around the time of the full moon.

30. Has this a Masonic significance?

No, it was simply so that members might travel to and from the lodge and their homes in more light.

31. Lodges have no numbers in only one Grand Jurisdiction in the United States. Which one is this?

Massachusetts.

32. In one Grand Jurisdiction in the United States there are about a dozen lodges with numbers, but no names. Which one?

Pennsylvania.

33. In all but one Grand Jurisdiction in the United States the Grand Master is given the title "Most Worshipful" and the other Grand Officers are usually "Right Worshipful." Which Grand Jurisdiction gives the Grand Master the title of "Right Worshipful" also?

Pennsylvania.

34. May a Masonic lodge adjourn?

No. The Master is the sole judge of the proper period at which the labors of the lodge should be terminated. Adjournment is a method used only in deliberative bodies, such as a Grand Lodge which does not confer degrees.

35. Why does the Master of a lodge wear a hat?

To uncover the head in the presence of superiors has been, among all Christian nations, held as a mark of respect. The converse of this is also true. To keep the head covered, while all around are uncovered, is a mark of superiority of rank or office.

36. What form of government does a Masonic lodge have?

Democratic.

37. Why is it democratic?

Because the members decide by ballot, or voting, who will be the principal officers.

38. Are all Masonic bodies democratic in structure?

No, the Scottish Rite is an hierarchy because the officers of the Supreme Body are not elected by the membership at large, but by those who have been elected to the Supreme Body.

39. We are accustomed to see the Master of a lodge sit in the East and the Wardens in the West and South. Is there another arrangement?

Yes, in many continental lodges, the Wardens sit in the West—one at each corner of the triangle with the apex in the East. Also true in some Scottish lodges.

40. Does a lodge under dispensation have the same powers as a regularly constituted lodge?

No. The powers of a U.D. lodge are strictly limited. It does not assume the status of a regular lodge until it is consecrated, dedicated and constituted by the Grand Master and officers, or those he delegates for the ceremony.

41. Are lodge officers elected or appointed?

In some jurisdictions all officers in the "line" are elected; in others, only the Master, Senior and Junior Wardens, Secretary and Treasurer are elected while the others are appointed.

42. How long do officers serve?

The usual term is one year, but nothing prevents re-election to the same office unless the by-laws so state.

43. Why are secretaries and treasurers often re-elected over a long period of years?

A good secretary serves as a connecting link between different administrations and makes for stability and smooth running. The same is true of the treasurer.

44. Is the position of the altar the same in all Masonic lodges?

No. In English lodges there is no central altar but a pedestal is placed immediately before the Worshipful Master.

45. Why is one prevented from passing between the altar and the Master in the East?

So that the Master's view of the Great Lights on the altar will not be obstructed.

46. What can the Master do if he sees a brother traversing this space thoughtlessly?

He can rise from his chair and walk to one side until the brother has passed.

47. In early times how was attendance at lodge enforced?

By fines. The by-laws of the early lodges contain lists of fines to be imposed for absence, swearing, and drunkenness.

48. Can a lodge move from place to place?

There is no mention made in the Ancient Landmarks or Regulations which forbids a lodge, upon the vote of the majority, from removing to a new location in the same city or town. The Constitution of the Grand Lodge or the by-laws of the lodge may, however, prohibit this without dispensation from the Grand Master, later confirmed by the Grand Lodge. However, a lodge may not move to another city or town without such dispensation and confirmation because the Charter of the lodge specifically names the town or city where the lodge was chartered.

49. Who presides in a Masonic lodge if the Master is absent?

The Senior Warden and if he is also absent, the Junior Warden presides.

50. If the Master and both Wardens are absent, who presides?

Generally, the lodge could not be opened unless by special dispensation.

51. Who is the intermediary between the Grand Master and the lodge?

The District Deputy Grand Master in most jurisdictions in the United States. He is the official representative of the Grand Master.

52. Who has charge of preparing the lodge room for the communication?

The Tiler.

53. Who are the paid officers of a lodge in the United States?

Generally, the Secretary, Tiler, Treasurer and Organist only.

54. Who are technically in charge of refreshments for the lodge?

The Stewards.

55. What officer presides in the lodge when on refreshment?

The Junior Warden.

56. In English lodges when the Master is absent who presides?

The Immediate Past Master takes the chair.

57. Are the "Lesser Lights" arranged the same in all jurisdictions?

No, there are ten or twelve placements of the three lights.

58. What types of lights are used for the "Lesser Lights"?

Candles, Gas, or Electric.

59. Do all lodges open the Bible at the same passages for the three degrees?

No, some Grand Lodges specify definite passages, others, among them New Jersey, do not.

60. Since the publication of Webb's *Monitor* what passages are usually used?

1st Degree: Psalms 133:1-3; 2nd Degree: Amos 7:7-9; 3rd Degree: Eccles. 12:1-7.

61. What are the usual passages from the Bible used in English lodges?

1st Degree: Ruth 4:7; 2nd Degree: Judges 12:6; 3rd Degree: I Kings 7:13-14.

62. Which is correct DEMIT or DIMIT?

Either is correct. This is a paper certifying a withdrawal from a lodge or Masonic body when in good standing.

63. Is it necessary to present a demit, or dimit, to a lodge upon affiliation?

Yes, the document must be presented and cancelled on its face before membership is consummated.

64. What becomes of the demit, or dimit, after affiliation?

It becomes the property of the lodge, or Masonic body in which affiliation is made.

65. Do all jurisdictions confer degrees for each other?

No. Pennsylvania will confer none. California, Colorado, Delaware, Indiana, Nevada, South Carolina, and Wyoming will only confer the second and third degrees. However, these regulations are subject to change by action of the various Grand Lodges.

66. How long may a brother wait between any two degrees in a lodge?

Regulations differ. In some jurisdictions there is a specified time. Some instances of great length are: Stephen J. Thorn of Warren Lodge No. 32, Schultzville, New York, was initiated October 27, 1883, passed December 13, 1883, but did not receive the Master Mason degree until July 17, 1930—46 years and 6 months later. Thomas Mortimer of Globe Lodge No. 113, Madison, Nebraska, received his E.A. degree on May 25, 1886, his F.C. on February 22, 1901, and his M.M. on March 21, 1921. Thus, he stood 34 years and 10 months between the Entered Apprentice and Master Mason degrees.

67. What is the Past Master's degree in the lodge?

The ceremony used in qualifying the Master after his election before he can preside. It is given under various names, but only fifteen Grand Lodges in the United States have the ceremony in use.

68. When does a man become a Past Master, or past officer, of any Masonic body?

The moment he is installed. However, some Grand Bodies legislate that in order to be a "Past" one must have served a certain length of time; in other bodies, he must have actually "passed the chair," that is, he must no longer hold the office.

69. Are there any cases where one who presides in a Masonic body does not hold a title of "Past"?

Yes, but in such cases he is usually "emeritus."

70. If a brother, who was not a Past Master in his lodge, becomes Master of a Research Lodge, does he become a Past Master of the jurisdiction?

Yes. And if the Research Lodge is in a jurisdiction where the Past Master, or Qualifying Degree, is conferred on incoming Masters, he must be given this degree in the usual form for that jursidiction before being installed as Master of the Research Lodge.

71. Does this also hold true of the presiding officer in a Chapter of Research?

Yes, in the same manner and proviso as in the lodge.

72. What is the name of the official officer of the lodge in foreign Grand Jurisdictions which is seldom heard of in the United States?

The Immediate Past Master.

73. Who conducts the funeral services for a deceased Mason?

The lodge should properly conduct such a service. However, there is no reason why another branch of Freemasonry cannot conduct such a service if requested by the family of the deceased.

74. What two Saints John's Days are celebrated by Freemasons?

Saint John, the Baptist, on June 24th; Saint John, the Evangelist, on December 27th.

75. Why these particular dates?

The summer and winter solstices occur at these times, and Masonry illustrates a cycle of life (time).

76. Why are cornerstones laid in the northeast corner?

Because the northeast is the point of beginning, midway between the darkness of the North and the light of the East.

77. Is it just as much a violation to wrong or defraud a non-Mason as it is a Mason?

Yes, there is nothing in Masonry which justifies two codes of conduct.

78. What is meant by "Masonic Customs"?

"Customs of the Masons," so often mentioned in Craft records, were not customs in the sense of fashions or habits, but were *laws* in the sense of common law.

79. Who is entitled to organized relief or charity of the lodge or Grand Lodge?

A Master Mason only, according to Masonic law, but Masonic practice gives relief to many in the spirit of brotherly love.

80. How may a Grand Lodge be organized?

It is universally recognized as the law of Masonry in the United States that whenever three or more chartered lodges in any State, or Territory, in which there is no existent Grand Lodge, meet in convention, they may organize a Grand Lodge for that State or Territory.

81. Is this true in other countries?

Mostly, but should a Grand Lodge be formed in some part of the British Empire, where lodges exist under the Grand Lodges of England, Ireland or Scotland, some of these lodges might continue under their original aegis.

82. Are there anachronisms in the Masonic ritual?

Yes, many. In the M.M. degree an instrument not made until hundreds of years after the time of King Solomon (the striking clock) is used. The Celestial and Terrestial Globes on the tops of the pillars are "out of time" as the world was considered flat during the period of our ritual setting. "Print, paint . . . or engrave" is an anachronism because printing and engraving were unknown until after the 14th century.

83. Are there any instances of Masonic lodges being "degree mills"?

Yes. From March 15, 1842, under a dispensation granted to Nauvoo Lodge, U.D., Nauvoo, Illinois, until August 11, 1842, (149 days) two hundred and eighty-six received all three degrees in the lodge. Two additional dispensations were granted by this same Grand Lodge the following year: Helm Lodge, U.D. and Nye Lodge, U.D. In one year these three lodges raised 1500 Masons. The Grand Lodge of Illinois then brought a speedy end to this practice the following year. Mother Kilwinning Lodge No. 0, in Edinburgh, Scotland, has more petitions every year than any other lodge in the world. As an example, in 1920, they enrolled 384 new members including 176 affiliations.

84. What is wrong with the following: "All the implements of Masonry indiscriminately, but more especially the trowel"?

The word "but" should not be used.

85. Which is proper: The Lodge was opened IN or ON the _____ degree?

The Lodge was opened ON the _____ degree.

PART VII

Symbolism and Philosophy

1. What are the primary purposes of Freemasonry?

To enlighten the mind, arouse the conscience, stimulate the noble and generous impulses of the human heart. It seeks to promote the best type of manhood based upon the practice of Brotherly Love and the Golden Rule. In short, to make good men better.

2. What is the symbolic covering of the lodge?

A celestial canopy, or starry-decked heaven.

3. What are the ornaments of a lodge?

The Mosaic Pavement, the Indented Tessel, and the Blazing Star.

4. Name the furnishings of the lodge.

The Holy Bible, Square and Compasses, together with a Charter or Dispensation.

5. What two sciences have always been held in special reverence by Freemasons?

Geometry and Astronomy, the latter because it underlies the former.

6. Where were the "fixed lights"?

In the East, West and South. The old rituals called them the "fixed lights" and their use was said to be "to light the men to, at, and from their work."

7. What is a "lewis"?

An instrument made use of by Operative Masons to lift heavy stones and, symbolically, a symbol of strength. The more common meaning is the name applied to the son of a Mason who becomes a member of the Craft before he reaches the usual age. In the United States it is used mostly in Pennsylvania.

8. Name the seven Liberal Arts and Sciences.

Grammar, Rhetoric, Logic, Arithmetic, Geometry, Music, and Astronomy.

9. Name the Five Orders of Architecture.

Doric, Ionic, Corinthian, Tuscan, and Composite.

10. Name several emblems, or symbols, of Freemasonry.

The Ark, Hourglass, Sprig of Acacia, Beehive, Square and Compasses, Spade, Mosaic Tables, 47th Problem of Euclid, The Anchor, Jacob's Ladder, Moon and the Stars.

11. Why is the Sprig of Acacia used as an emblem in Freemasonry?

It probably originated because of a Jewish custom of planting a branch of *acacia vera* (gum arabic plant) on the grave of a departed relative. It symbolizes Masonry's great doctrine, the immortality of the soul.

12. What is the All-Seeing Eye?

An emblem in the degree of Master Mason, reminding us of the superintending Providence perceiving the most secret things.

13. What was used as a symbol of the Christians in the early years?

A fish. The Greek word comprised the first letters of Jesus Christ, God's Son, Savior.

14. What general symbol is used by Freemasonry?

The trowel.

15. Why is the Beehive emblematic of Freemasonry?

It is the perfect emblem of the power of industry; what no one bee, or succession of individual bees, could accomplish, is easy when hundreds of them work together at one task at one time.

16. What is the legend of the Winding Stairs?

An allegory to teach us the ascent of the mind from ignorance, through all the toils and study and the difficulties of obtaining knowledge, gleaning a little along the way and thus adding to our stock of knowledge at each step until the reward of how to seek God and His truth is gained in the full fruition of manhood (the middle chamber of life).

17. What is the symbolic meaning of the Setting Maul?

The Maul was a mallet used to tap a finished stone into place; hence, it came to symbolize the completing of a piece of work. In the Master Mason degree there are two mauls, the second being a weapon with a different meaning.

18. What is Masonic Charity?

It does not mean only the giving of alms for physical relief, but also charity of thought, often the more difficult.

19. What is the symbolic meaning of the Two Pillars?

One signifies strength or power which may be used wisely, or otherwise. The other pillar signifies establishment, control, or choice. Hence, in Freemasonry the brother passes between the two and the lesson learned is that strength, or power, without control is dangerous, and control without power is futile. It is a complement of the two which will enable him to climb the stairway of life by strength, but directed by control, or wisdom.

20. What is the symbolism of the "step" in Masonry?

Respect for the altar from which Masonic light emanates. It teaches symbolically that the passage from darkness and ignorance of life is through death to light and knowledge of the eternal life.

21. What symbolizes the "Rough Ashlar"?

The member as yet unpracticed in the arts which he is expected to pursue.

22. What symbolizes the "Perfect Ashlar"?

The mental and moral development of the individual that he may become acceptable in the sight of God.

23. What is the symbolism of the 3, 5, and 7 steps?

The stairs as a whole are a representation of life—the mental and spiritual life gained by studying, learning and enlarging one's mental horizons. Freemasons divide the fifteen steps into three, referring to the officers of a lodge; five, concerned with the Orders of Architecture and the human senses; seven, concerned with the Liberal Arts and Sciences.

24. There are many interpretations of the symbolism of the Third degree. What are some of them?

(1) That the degree, as a whole, is a symbol of old age, of experience, wisdom and the preparation for the life to come. (2) That truth and what is good will always overcome evil. (3) That ignorance and brute force can destroy virtue. (4) Perhaps the most universally accepted symbolic interpretation is the immortality of the soul.

25. Masonry has been described as a "system of morality veiled in allegory and illustrated by symbols." Why is it so veiled?

A definition is limited and confining. Allegories and symbols are infinite in their application and each Mason is therefore enabled to read into such allegories and symbols his own individual interpretation, each to the limit of his capacity. Thus, men of many minds can read into the words of the ceremony their own concept of the underlying truth, to find, perhaps, that particular lesson then needed most. As knowledge increases, one gains a still wider vision and meaning.

26. What is the symbolic meaning of "Darkness"?

Ignorance. Freemasonry seeks to enlighten the candidate and thus rescue him from a darkened world.

27. Are Masonic penalties symbolic, or may they be enforced?

The only Masonic penalty inflicted by the Craft upon a traitor is the scorn and detestation of the Craft whom he has sought to betray.

28. Does this particular wording of the obligation vary in other jurisdictions?

Yes, in Irish lodges the candidate "bears in mind the ancient penalty." It is referred to as the *symbolic* penalty.

29. What is the symbolic history of the Pillars of the Porch?

It is supposed that Solomon had reference to the pillar of cloud and the pillar of fire which went before the Israelites in the wilderness. Thus, in passing through the pillars, the Jews were reminded of the abundant promises of God and were inspired with confidence in His protection.

30. Why do Masons come from the "Lodge of the Holy Saints John of Jerusalem"?

According to Masonic tradition, the first lodge was held at Jerusalem and dedicated to St. John, the Baptist, later to St. John, the Evangelist, and finally to both. From this lodge all other lodges are supposed to have descended.

73

31. What is the symbolic meaning of the "flaming sword"?

A sword with a spiral, or twisted, blade is known as a flaming sword. The flaming sword of the Tiler refers to the sword which guarded the entrance to Paradise.

32. What is the symbolic use of the "working tools"?

That if we win the crown for which we strive, it will not be because we have used our working tools in the erection of bridges, factories and buildings, but it will be because we have taken the plans and specifications of the Great Architect and have followed with scrupulous care the blue print which He drew for the greatest of all structures, that of human brotherhood.

33. What is the difference between an emblem and a symbol?

An emblem is a representation or visible sign of an idea. A symbol compares one thing with another.

34. What is the symbolic meaning of the pomegranate?

Plenty, because of its many seeds.

35. What is the symbolic meaning of the Swastika?

The name comes from the Sanskrit words meaning "well being." The true Swastika goes sunwise (clockwise) and the false one goes anti-clockwise. The symbol adopted by the Nazis was of the latter. All swastikas are evolved from the cross formation.

PART VIII

Royal Arch

1. Where do we first hear of Royal Arch Masonry?

In England in the 1720's and 1730's there are several instances where Royal Arch terms are used, but the word "chapter" meant "head" and it is not claimed that a Chapter of Royal Arch Masons was intended. There was no doubt an acquaintance with what we now recognize as the Royal Arch story.

2. What is the earliest date that can be claimed as Royal Arch working as we know it today?

1743. Lodge No. 21 in Youghal, County Cork, Ireland, had a St. John's Day in Winter procession and it was reported in the *Dublin Journal* "that The Royall Arch was carried by two Excellent Masons." There is some evidence to show that there was in existence, in Scotland, Stirling Rock Royal Arch Lodge in July, 1743. If all doubt could be removed then this would make the Scottish Lodge or Chapter the oldest in the world.

3. Where is the first actual record of the conferring of the Royal Arch degree in the United States?

In the lodge at Fredericksburg, Virginia, on December 22, 1753.

4. Was George Washington a Royal Arch Mason?

There is no record that he ever received the degree.

5. What are the names of the degrees in Royal Arch Masonry in the United States?

Mark Master, Past Master, Most Excellent Master, and Royal Arch.

6. Which two of these are of American origin?

The Past Master and the Most Excellent Master degrees.

7. Which Grand Chapter in the United States does not confer the Past Master degree in its chapters?

Pennsylvania.

8. What is done when a visitor from a Pennsylvania chapter visits a chapter in another jurisdiction for the first time?

He is "healed," that is, he is obligated in the Past Master degree.

9. What is the Order of Anointed High Priests?

A ceremony, or degree, usually controlled by an independent "Convention of Anointed High Priests" who confer the degree on those who have been elected to serve as High Priests in Royal Arch chapters.

10. Who is credited with forming the American Chapter system of degrees conferred in Royal Arch Masonry?

Thomas Smith Webb. This, however, has not been proved.

11. In what year was, what is now known as, the General Grand Chapter of Royal Arch Masons formed?

In 1797.

12. Are all Grand Chapters in the United States affiliated with the General Grand Chapter?

No.

13. How often does the General Grand Chapter meet?

Every three years.

14. What is the general emblem of Royal Arch Masonry?

The triple tau within a triangle and circle.

15. Of what is the Royal Arch banner composed?

It consists of ancient astronomical emblems.

16. What is the color of the borders of Royal Arch aprons?

Scarlet, or red.

17. When fully clothed, what does the High Priest wear that no other presiding officer in Masonry wears?

A breastplate with stones denoting the Twelve Tribes of Israel.

18. What do the upright and horizontal lines forming a cross on the Royal Arch banner denote?

The equator cut at right angles by the solstitial colure.

19. Of the Twelve Tribes of Israel, which returned under Zerubbabel?

Two, those of Judah and Benjamin, according to one Biblical version.

20. What is the difference in rank of the first two officers of a chapter in the United States and in England?

The High Priest presides in the United States which is a democracy. In England it is the First Grand Principal (King).

21. There are several differences in English and United States chapters. What are some of these differences?

(1) An English R.A. chapter must be attached to an existing Craft lodge under the control of the United Grand Lodge. (2) The precedence of a chapter is determined by the date of the lodge and not by its own date of constitution. (3) Any brother who has received the Master Mason degree is eligible for the Royal Arch. (4) Very seldom is the candidate obliged to "pass the veils" as a preliminary to his exaltation, although in the early English ceremonies the candidate was required to pass *three* veils. (5) The Mark degree follows the Royal Arch.

22. In the lodge the members are called "brothers," but in the chapter they are called what?

Companions.

23. How is the Royal Arch Year calculated?

By adding 530 to the current year.

24. What is the meaning of the name "Moses," the lawgiver of the Jews, who plays such an important part in the ritual of Royal Arch Masonry?

It is derived from the Egyptian word *ms'* (meaning son) and is connected with the Hebrew word *māshah* (meaning to draw out). The name is doubly fitting since Moses was drawn from the water and was adopted as a son by Pharaoh's daughter.

25. Is JeHoVaH the sacred word?

No, it is a Rabbinical perversion of it, formed by the insertion of vowels which do not belong to it.

26. Who was struck dead for merely touching the Ark of the Covenant?

Uzzah. (II Samuel 6:7)

27. Who were Korah, Dathan and Abiram?

Descendants of Reuben who conspired against Moses and Aaron saying, "Ye take too much upon you." (Num. 16:3)

28. In what Masonic order do we find Melchizedek the prominent character?

The Order of High Priesthood.

29. What is said to have been the shape of the keystone used in buildings by the earliest Aryan builders?

Tau shaped; the wedge shaped keystone; although of old date, is of a more modern form.

30. What was the figure traced upon the doorposts of the faithful among the Jews to save them from slaughter?

The Tau cross.

31. What three figures are embraced in the Tau?

Right angles, horizontals, and perpendiculars. The triple tau is literally three taus. Tau is the nineteenth letter in the Greek alphabet and the twentieth in the English alphabet; it is our "T."

32. Why is a circle inscribed in the Masonic keystone?

A circle is the astronomical sign and Egyptian hieroglyph of the sun. It is placed in the keystone to denote the sun in the summer solstice exalted to the summit of the zodiacal arch.

33. What is the Catenarian Arch?

Catena is the Latin for "chain" and the Catenarian Arch has a curve the same as that assumed by a chain or heavy rope suspended between two points.

34. What is the Hexalpha?

Interlaced triangles forming the six-pointed star.

35. What is the Hexalpha more commonly called?

The Shield of David or the Seal of Solomon.

36. What is the five-pointed star called?

The Pentalpha or Morning Star. The Pentalpha is not the Royal Arch jewel of today but undoubtedly in earlier days it was the jewel of the "Antients" part of the Royal Arch.

37. What were the Israelitish standards?

The Man, the Lion, the Ox, and the Eagle.

38. To what tribes of Israel were they assigned?

To Reuben, Judah, Ephraim, and Dan, respectively.

39. To what did the figures of a man, a lion, an ox, and an eagle, used as standards, refer?

To understanding, or wisdom; power; patient administration; and swiftness, respectively, in executing commands of the Most High.

40. What is the first and simplest form possible in geometry of which all other forms are composed?

The triangle.

41. What is the symbolic meaning of the chisel in the Mark Master degree?

The effect of knowledge or education on the mind.

42. What is the symbolic meaning of the crow?

A crow is an iron bar used to raise heavy objects. It is one of the working tools of the Royal Arch and symbolically teaches the candidate to raise his thoughts above the corrupting influence of worldly matters.

43. What is the meaning of Rabboni?

Chief Builder, or Supreme Architect.

44. Were the three highest officers in the American Chapter always called the High Priest, King and Scribe?

No, an early record (1769) of St. Andrew's Chapter in Boston lists the officers as Master, Senior Warden, and Junior Warden.

45. Why did all ancient buildings contain a system of mason's marks?

They were common to the generality of the trades and were used to show by whom the work was done.

46. Why is the High Priest said to have had a rope tied about his waist when he entered the Holy of Holies once each year?

That he might be pulled out in case of sudden death. No one but the High Priest was allowed to enter under penalty of death.

47. Distinguish between Hiram, King of Tyre, and Hiram Abif.

Hiram, King of Tyre, reigned for 34 years. He was friend of both Solomon and Solomon's father, David. He supplied the cedars, masons and carpenters for building of the Temple. Hiram Abif was an artificer, whose father was a Tyrian and his mother a widow of Naphtali, but by birth a woman of Dan. Hiram Abif contributed his knowledge to the bronze or copper work in connection with Solomon's Temple.

48. Distinguish between an Actual Past Master and a Virtual Past Master.

An Actual Past Master is one who has served as Master of his lodge. A Virtual Past Master is one who has had the Past Master degree in the Royal Arch, but who has not been elected or has not served as Master of a lodge.

49. What qualification was originally required before taking the Royal Arch degree?

That the candidate be a Past Master. As this restricted membership to those who had actually served as Master of a lodge, the qualification was abandoned and the ceremony of "passing the chair" adopted.

50. Is it necessary for a Mason to be a member of the Templar Orders before he can be a Royal Arch Mason?

No, in the United States it is just the reverse.

51. What Grand Jurisdiction has never been a member of the General Grand Chapter or the General Grand Council of Royal and Select Masters?

Virginia, because the Grand Chapter of Virginia controls the Royal and Select degrees and they are conferred in the chapter.

52. Where was the first Grand Chapter organized?

In England, in 1767, by Lord Blayney, Grand Master of the Premier Grand Lodge.

53. Where was the first Grand Chapter organized in the United States?

Hartford, Connecticut, in 1798.

54. How many states were represented at this formation?

Four: Massachusetts, Rhode Island, New York, and Connecticut.

55. What qualification, aside from those usual in all Masonic bodies, is necessary before one may become a Royal Arch Mason?

He must be a member in good standing of a Symbolic lodge.

56. What are the degrees of the Chapter called?

Capitular degrees.

57. Who has been given credit for originating the term "capitular"?

Albert G. Mackey, of South Carolina, U.S.A.

PART IX

Royal and Select Master

1. Where and when do we first hear of the Council degrees?

Circa 1790 in Maryland, New York, and New Jersey. The first account of a council of Royal and Select Masters is 1810 in New York.

2. How many degrees constitute the Council?

Three: Royal Master, Select Master, and Super-Excellent Master.

3. The degrees of the lodge are called "Symbolic." What are those of the Council called?

Cryptic degrees.

4. Which one of the Cryptic degrees is not obligatory in some states?

The Super-Excellent Master.

5. There is an Order, usually independent from Grand Councils, in the Cryptic Rite having the same position in the Rite as the Anointed Order of High Priesthood has in the Capitular Rite. What is it?

The Order of the Silver Trowel, or Anointed Order of Kings. It is the Thrice Illustrious Master degree.

6. What council was largely responsible for the formation of Cryptic Masonry?

Columbian Council No. 1, New York, N.Y.

7. It is known that Columbian Council No. 1 also conferred degrees which never became a part of the Cryptic Rite. Name some of these degrees.

Knight of the Round Table; Knight of the Honorable Order of the Garter, or Order of St. George of Capidosia.

8. When and where was the first Grand Council formed?

In 1819, in Connecticut.

9. When did the General Grand Council come into being?

March 1, 1881.

10. How often does the General Grand Council meet?

Once every three years at the time of the General Grand Chapter meeting.

11. Who is given credit for having taken the Council degrees and formed them into a recognized Masonic rite?

Jeremy L. Cross.

12. Who is thought to have originated the term "cryptic"?

Rob Morris.

13. What is the Cryptic Rite color?

Purple.

14. In what jurisdictions do the members of the Cryptic Rite wear triangular aprons?

New Jersey; also, in three Canadian jurisdictions.

15. What is the emblem of Cryptic Masonry?

A broken triangle.

16. What other Masonic emblem is often used with the broken triangle?

The trowel.

17. What qualification, aside from those usual in all Masonic bodies, is necessary before one may become a Royal and Select Master?

He must be a member in good standing in a Royal Arch chapter.

18. What is the name of the presiding officer of a council?

Thrice Illustrious Master, or Illustrious Master.

19. What is the name of the lowest council officer?

The Sentinel.

20. How do we arrive at the Cryptic Masonic date?

By adding 1000 to the current year.

21. What is this date called?

Anno Depositionis, meaning In the Year of the Deposit and is abbreviated A. Dep.

22. What three companions formed a number of bodies of either the Select Master or Royal Master degrees previous to the formation of the Rite?

Jeremy L. Cross, James Cushman, and John Barker.

23. Are the Cryptic degrees worked in countries other than the United States?

Yes. In England there are four Cryptic degrees which are Most Excellent Master, Royal Master, Secret Master, and Super-Excellent Master. They are also found in most English-speaking countries.

PART X

Knights Templar

1.   Are the medieval Knights Templar connected with the modern Knights Templar?

No. Many writers have written articles claiming such a succession, but historical research has developed no such verification.

2.   When do we first hear of modern Knights Templar?

In the latter part of the 18th century in the British Isles.

3.   What is the first record found of the conferring of the Order of the Temple in the United States?

In St. Andrew's Royal Arch Chapter at Boston, Massachusetts, August 28, 1769, on a William Davis.

4.   Are the grades conferred in the commandery known as degrees?

No, they are called "orders." In all knighthoods, the grades are so-called.

5.   What are the orders of the commandery called?

Chivalric orders.

6.   What are the grades conferred in the commanderies in the United States?

Order of the Red Cross, Knight Templar, and Knight of Malta.

7.   Which is correct: Knights Templar, Knight Templars, or Knights Templars?

Knights Templar.

8. Symbolic bodies are called lodges, Capitular bodies are called chapters, Cryptic bodies are called councils, but what are they called in the Chivalric orders?

Commanderies.

9. What is the National Grand Body of Knights Templar called in the United States?

The Grand Encampment of Knights Templar.

10. When was the Grand Encampment of the United States formed?

June 20, 1816, in New York City.

11. Until Grand Commanderies were formed, in what bodies were the Templar orders conferred?

In Royal Arch chapters, and before that, in lodges.

12. In the early years several other orders were conferred in addition to the Order of the Temple. Name some of them.

Red Cross of Babylon, Knight of Patmos, Christian Mark, Knight of the Holy Sepulchre, Mediterranean Pass, Knight of the Roman Eagle, Knight of Jericho, Royal Master.

13. Although the Grand Encampment continues to control the three orders, which one of them has no place in Christian knighthood?

The Order of the Red Cross.

14. Has it ever been suggested that the Grand Encampment cease conferring this order?

Yes, several times, but although it has been discussed and voted on at many of the Grand Encampment meetings, it has never been abolished.

15. Some claim that Chivalric Masonry is not Freemasonry. Why?

Because only Christians are admitted.

16. In what jurisdiction is it necessary to be a Royal and Select Master before joining a commandery?

None.

17. What degrees of Freemasonry are necessary in order to be made a Knight Templar?

Those of the lodge and the chapter.

18. Is there a grade in the commandery comparable to the Past Master degree in the lodge, the Past High Priest degree in the chapter, and the Past Thrice Illustrious Master degree in the council?

Yes, it is the Holy Royal Arch Knight Templar Priest, but it is not conferred in connection with commanderies. It is a separate order, and membership is by invitation only. This body is composed of Past Commanders.

19. What is "the accolade"?

A portion of a ceremony in conferring knighthood, now performed by touching the shoulders and head with a sword.

20. What was the "Beauseant"?

A war banner of the ancient Templars which was composed of black and white and used in the Order of the Temple.

21. Who was the first Grand Master of the Grand Encampment?

DeWitt Clinton, who served three terms: 1816 until his death on February 11, 1828.

22. Did any Grand Master serve longer?

Yes, William Blackstone Hubbard, the 5th Grand Master of the Grand Encampment, KT, who served four terms: from 1847 to 1859.

23. What is the color of the uniform of a Knight of Malta?

Black.

24. What is the color of the uniform of a Knight Templar?

White.

25. What subject has been under more or less constant discussion in Templary in the United States?

The uniform, because there has never been a general agreement as to what it should be. For the first forty years the Grand Encampment used no uniform. When it was finally adopted, it was the Civil War naval officer's uniform and was already obsolete as such.

26. Why is the white uniform of a Knight Templar not worn in the Commandery in the United States?

Simply because the Grand Encampment never adopted it, but rather adopted one for the body as used by the Malta Knights.

27. What jewel is obligatory on the uniform of a Knight Templar?

The jewel of the Order of Malta.

28. What is a crosier?

The staff of the Prelate.

29. What is the name of the presiding officer of a commandery?

Commander.

30. How many commanderies within a jurisdiction are required before they can unite to form a Grand Commandery where there is no such Grand Body?

Three commanderies.

31. What are the Grand Bodies in other countries called?

Great Priories.

32. What are the subordinate bodies in these countries called?

Preceptories.

PART XI

Scottish Rite

1. Where was the Scottish Rite formed in the United States?

In Charleston, South Carolina, on May 31, 1801.

2. Who presided at this meeting?

John Mitchell and he remained the presiding officer of the Rite until his death on January 25, 1816, at Charleston.

3. Who is supposed to have written the original constitutions of the Scottish Rite?

Frederick the Great, of Germany, but historically, this has never been proved.

4. From what country did the degrees of the Scottish Rite probably originate?

France. Chevalier de Bonneville, of the College of Jesuits of Clermont, Paris, in 1754, formed a chapter consisting of twenty-five degrees.

5. How does the Rite get the name "Scottish"?

One of these degrees founded in France was called "Scottish Master." The chapter no doubt had Scots Masters in its membership and when the Supreme Council was organized in Charleston, the name "Scottish Rite" was adopted for these degrees.

6. Had any of these degrees ever been conferred before a Supreme Council of the Thirty-third Degree was organized?

Yes, most of them in some Masonic body. The Supreme Council was made up of degrees taken from various rites.

7. What is the earliest record of any of the grades being conferred in the United States?

December 20, 1767, when a Lodge of Perfection was opened in Albany, New York.

8. How long did the Supreme Council headquarters remain in Charleston?

Until 1870 when it was moved to Washington, D.C.

9. We have two Supreme Councils in the United States. How did this happen?

E. De La Motte, a Special Deputy Representative, and others, from the Supreme Grand Council at Charleston, opened a new body by letters-patent in New York, on August 5, 1813.

10. What are the names of the two Supreme Councils, and where are their respective headquarters?

"The Ancient and Accepted Rite of Scottish Rite Freemasonry" in the Southern Jurisdiction, having headquarters in Washington, D.C., and "Ancient Accepted Scottish Rite of Freemasonry" in the Northern Jurisdiction, with headquarters at Boston, Massachusetts.

11. Were there other bodies set up in opposition to the Scottish Rite?

Yes, several. The most noted are those called the Cerneau Rite, headed by Joseph Cerneau of New York. Remnants of these Cerneau bodies were still active in the early 20th century.

12. What was the "Rite of Memphis"?

Another Masonic rite which was set up in opposition to the Scottish Rite in the United States.

13. Is this Rite still active?

No. It was finally taken over by the Grand College of Rites of the United States which controls it but does not confer the grades, as is the case with a number of dormant Masonic rites once conferred in the United States.

14. Did the Rite of Memphis have a large membership?

Yes, at one time it had more members than the Scottish Rite.

15. In the Northern Jurisdiction there were several groups claiming to be the proper one for regular recognition. What eventually became of them?

At Boston, Massachusetts, on May 17, 1867, all factions came together and signed an "Oath of Fealty" after it was administered by the M.P. Sov. Grand Commander, John L. Lewis.

16. Who became the first Grand Commander at the election at this meeting?

Josiah H. Drummond, of Maine, who continued in office until September 17, 1879.

17. Who was instrumental in reviving the Scottish Rite in the United States after it had reached a very low ebb in both membership and activity?

Albert Pike, of Arkansas.

18. There is a decoration in the Southern Jurisdiction which precedes the granting of the Honorary Thirty-third Degree. What is it?

Knight Commander of the Court of Honor. (KCCH)

19. What are the requirements for any Mason to become a Scottish Rite Mason in the United States?

That he be a Master Mason in good standing.

20. Does the Scottish Rite confer the first three degrees of Freemasonry?

Not in the United States as this would be an infringement on the Symbolic lodge.

21. What is the general emblem of the Scottish Rite?

The double headed eagle.

22. What is the meaning of the double headed eagle?

Double jurisdiction. The Council of Emperors of the East and West, established in Paris in 1758, adopted this emblem, this Council claiming double jurisdiction.

23. What is a Consistory?

The meetings of members of the Thirty-second degree.

24. What is the motto of the 32°?

Spes mea in Deo est (My Hope is in God). (N. Juris.) *In hoc signo vinces* (In this sign we conquer). (S. Juris.)

25. What is the 33°?

A degree conferred by the Supreme Council of the Scottish Rite in both Southern and Northern jurisdictions. It cannot be petitioned for; it is conferred for outstanding merit.

Note: Nos. 26 to 59,
inclusive, apply to Northern Jurisdiction

26. What are the Ineffable degrees?

4° to 14°, inclusive, and are conferred in a Lodge of Perfection. The word "ineffable" means inexpressible, too sacred for utterance. Masonically, the ineffable degrees treat of the Ineffable Name of the Great Jehovah, and of His Ineffable Essence.

27. What are the Second Temple degrees?

15⁰ to 16⁰, inclusive, conferred in a Council of Princes of Jerusalem.

28. What are the Spiritual Temple degrees?

17⁰ and 18⁰, conferred in a Chapter of the Rose Croix.

29. What are the Historical, Philosophic, and Chivalric degrees?

19⁰ to 32⁰, inclusive, conferred in a Consistory.

Ineffable Degrees

A brief description of each of the following:

30. 4⁰—SECRET MASTER

This pertains to King Solomon's Temple and the appointment of seven of the most worthy and expert Master Masons as special guardians of the Sanctum Sanctorum and of the sacred furniture. Secrecy, Silence, and Fidelity are taught in this degree.

31. 5⁰—PERFECT MASTER

Commemorates the death of GMHA and teaches that we should learn to pay due respect to the memory of a deceased worthy brother.

32. 6⁰—INTIMATE SECRETARY

King Solomon saves the life of a supposed spy, or eaves-dropper. The degree teaches zealousness, faithfulness, and that we should ever be careful not to offend a brother by prying into his secrets, and that "a soft answer turneth away wrath."

33. 7⁰—PROVOST AND JUDGE

In accordance with the legend of this degree, King Solomon found it necessary to appoint several judges upon the death of the slain Grand Master in order that justice might be administered among the workmen of the Temple. The degree teaches Justice, Equity, and Impartiality, that Justice should be administered with mercy.

34. 8⁰—INTENDANT OF THE BUILDING

The construction of the Temple having been stayed due to the death of the Chief Architect, King Solomon appointed five superintendents—one for each of the Five Departments of Architecture. Under their supervision the building progressed. The degree teaches the exercise and propagation of charity and benevolence, educating the orphan, comforting the sick and distressed.

35. 9⁰—MASTER ELECT OF NINE

Solomon elects nine to investigate so that the offenders may be brought to justice. The purpose of the degree is to inculcate and illustrate the lesson that we should be careful in not allowing ourselves to be led astray by an excess of zeal, even in a good cause, nor to take matters in our own hands to inflict punishment, even justly due, for the violation of human or divine laws.

36. 10⁰—MASTER ELECT OF FIFTEEN

A continuation in the series and recounts in detail the mode of the arrest and punishment of the remaining assassins. It reminds us that the unerring eye of Justice will discover the guilty and mete just punishment. Morally, it instructs us that ambition and fanaticism are overthrown and dispelled by the sword of Justice and Freedom.

37. 11⁰—SUBLIME MASTER ELECTED

The degree emblematically illustrates the reward conferred by King Solomon upon twelve of the Masters Elect of Fifteen who were instrumental in bringing to justice the assassins of the Master Builder, constituting them governors over the twelve tribes of Israel. The degree instructs that the true and faithful brother will, sooner or later, receive his just reward and teaches us to be Earnest, Honest, and Sincere.

38. 12⁰—GRAND MASTER ARCHITECT

This degree is alleged to have been established as a school of instruction for the workmen of the Temple, to assure uniformity in work, and to reward those eminent in science and skill. The rules of architecture and the connection of the liberal arts and sciences are amplified. The degree teaches that Virtue is as necessary as Talent.

39. 13⁰—MASTER OF THE NINTH ARCH

This degree forms the climax of the Ineffable Degrees; it is the keystone of the arch and discovers that which is revealed in the succeeding degree of Perfection.

40. 14⁰—GRAND, ELECT, PERFECT AND SUBLIME MASON

The lodge represents the Secret Vault under the Sanctum Sanctorum in which is the Pillar of Beauty, and on this is placed the Holy four-letter Name. This degree reveals and explains the Tetragrammaton. The degree teaches that when one has properly consecrated his life—mind and heart—for final preparation, that reward is achieved on the "completion of the Temple."

Historical, or Second Temple Degrees

41. 15⁰—KNIGHT OF THE EAST OR SWORD

Relates to the Babylonian captivity, the release and return of the captives to Jerusalem and the rebuilding of the Second Temple under authority given by King Cyrus. Its lesson teaches Fidelity to conviction.

42. 16⁰—PRINCE OF JERUSALEM

A continuation of the preceding degree representing the trials of the workers in the re-building of the Temple, and of their final success, aided by King Darius. Zerubbabel ordered that the men should work with the sword in one hand and a trowel in the other. The theme of this degree is the majesty of Truth.

Philosophical, or Spiritual Temple Degrees

43. 17⁰—KNIGHT OF THE EAST AND WEST

The Word is again lost and, figuratively, the Third Temple or Spiritual Temple—in the heart of man—is to be built and dedicated to the God of Truth. This degree is an introduction to the 18⁰.

44. 18⁰—KNIGHT OF THE ROSE CROIX

The novice is still in search of the Truth and the lost Word and, in his journeys through the years, he learns the three virtues which are to guide him: Faith, Hope and Charity, and he is taught the meaning of the New Law.

Historical and Philosophical Degrees

45. 19⁰—GRAND PONTIFF

The eleven degrees of the Areopagus which follow unfold the errors and frailties of human nature and instruct us how to overcome them. This degree protrays the conflict between good and evil. The sworn Knight of Justice, Truth, and Tolerance is admonished to be patient and work.

46. 20⁰—MASTER AD VITAM

The duties, powers and privileges of a Master. That the right to govern is not only through selection of the brethren, but by intelligence attained through patient labor and the study of Masonic doctrines. The requisites are Toleration, Justice, and Truth.

47. 21⁰—NOACHITE, OR PRUSSIAN KNIGHT

The story of the Crusaders who sought to shield and protect the innocent and, while rendering justice, to hold all guiltless until convicted.

48. 22⁰—PRINCE OF LIBANUS

Known also as Knight of the Royal Axe. The story tells of those who cut cedars on Mount Libanus for the building of the Ark for Noah. This degree teaches men that labor is honorable and that we should strive to improve the condition of the toiling millions. All are workmen whatever be their vocations, and rank and nobility are not excepted.

49. 23⁰—CHIEF OF THE TABERNACLE

Relates to the Tabernacle and its ancient ceremonies. Unholy sacrilege and presumptuous interference with sacred ceremonies are forbidden, and only those with hearts divested of all impurity are commended in the performance of holy rites.

50. 24°—PRINCE OF THE TABERNACLE

The special duties of a Prince of the Tabernacle are to labor incessantly for the glory of God, the honor of his country, and the happiness of his brethren, and to offer up thanks and prayers in lieu of sacrifices of flesh and blood.

51. 25°—KNIGHT OF THE BRAZEN SERPENT

Relates to the time when the camp of the Israelites was pitched at Punon after the death of Aaron, in the fortieth year of the wandering of the children of Israel in the wilderness. The duties of a Knight of the Brazen Serpent are to purify the soul of its alloy of earthliness and to restore faith in God.

52. 26°—PRINCE OF MERCY

When Domitian was emperor of Rome and when danger and death hung on their footsteps, the Christian Masons met in the Catacombs to celebrate the Mysteries. This degree, while depicting the mysteries as practised by the first Christians, shows that Masonry is of no one age, belongs to all time, is of no one religion, and finds its great truths in all.

53. 27°—KNIGHT COMMANDER OF THE TEMPLE

Dedicated to the Teutonic Knights of the House of St. Mary of Jerusalem. The Order originated at the siege of St. Jean d'Acre, when tents for the sick and wounded were made from the sails of ships. The Knights fought the infidel, Saladin, by day and nursed the sick by night and guarded the city of Jerusalem against the Saracens to protect Christendom. Their five excellent qualities were Humility, Temperance, Chastity, Generosity, and Honor.

54. 28°—KNIGHT OF THE SUN

This is the last of the philosophical degrees and its doctrine is derived from the *Kabala*. It treats of Science, Reason and Faith, Nature being the primary, consistent, and certain revelation of God.

55. 29⁰—KNIGHT OF ST. ANDREW

The degree intends to inculcate Equality and represents the Knight as the exponent of Truth. Toleration is exemplified in this, the last of the instructive degrees of the Historical and Philosphical series. It is a fitting climax to the theory of Universal Religion.

Chivalric Degrees

56. 30⁰—KNIGHT KADOSH

This and the following two degrees form the Templar degrees of the Ancient and Accepted Scottish Rite. The virtues of the Order are rehearsed and the reward for a due reverence of the obligations and observance of the vows and tenets of the Institution are exemplified. A Knight Kadosh proves himself practically a true defender of the Temple of the Most High God and, while armed with steel outwardly, he is inwardly armed with Faith and Love—Faith to God and Love for his fellowman.

57. 31⁰—GRAND INSPECTOR INQUISITOR COMMANDER

The practical test of the neophyte in the preceding degree is, in this one, changed to a thorough examination under charges against Masonic law and duty before the Order of the Five Brethren. Wise sayings of sages and law-givers are quoted for instruction. It teaches the administration of impartial justice with firmness, but ever remembering the frailty and imperfection of human nature, and to pardon and forgive while there yet remains hope of reformation.

58. 32⁰—SUBLIME PRINCE OF THE ROYAL SECRET

The degree was originally a Christian degree of Knighthood. Its object was, for a long time, to reconquer the Holy Land and plant the Banner of the Cross once more on the ruined walls of Jerusalem. It teaches that Masons should be diligent in their war against the ancient enemies of the human race—that they would be lovers of Wisdom and apostles of Liberty, Equality, and Fraternity.

59. 33⁰—SOVEREIGN GRAND INSPECTOR GENERAL

Conferred only by the Supreme Council which is the executive body of all Scottish Rite bodies. May not be petitioned for as this degree is given only for merit and is conferred as an honorarium.

60. How often does the Supreme Council convene?

The regular meetings in the Northern Jurisdiction are held each year. In the Southern Jurisdiction they are held every odd year.

61. Is inter-visitation by members of the various Scottish Rite jurisdictions permissible?

Yes, if proper credentials of membership are presented.

62. How many Thirty-third Degree Masons (Honorary) are there?

In 1948 the Northern Jurisdiction had 2,150; up to that year this honor had been conferred upon 5,620 brethren. In 1948 the Southern Jurisdiction had 2,551.

63. What are the Scottish Rite degrees called abroad?

Usually, "The Ancient and Accepted Rite," the original corporate title.

64. Albert Pike, famous Scottish Rite Mason, and Sovereign Grand Commander of the Southern Supreme Council for many years, is noted for compiling a book on that Rite of Freemasonry. What is the title?

Morals and Dogma, first published in 1871 and consisted of 861 pages.

65. In 1909 a much needed "Digest-Index" consisting of 218 pages was added. Who compiled this?

Trevanion William Hugo, of Minnesota.

66.   In the Northern Jurisdiction, the 20⁰ is known as the GEORGE WASHINGTON DEGREE. It was written by a newspaper man of San Antonio, Texas. What was his name?

J. Frank Davis, author of the play, *The Ladder.*

67.   What is the significance of the luminous pedestal displayed in Scottish Rite cathedrals?

A symbol of the light of Reason, given by God to man.

68.   What is the explanation of the "Blazing Star"?

In the 4^0, a symbol of the light of Divine Providence pointing out the way of truth. In the 9^0 it is called the "Star of Directions" which guides the pilgrim on his journey through life. In the 28^0 it is symbolic of a true Freemason, who, by advancing in knowledge and perfecting himself in the way of truth, becomes like a blazing star.

69.   Has the Supreme Council taken any definite stand on the American public school system in the United States?

Yes. The Supreme Council of the Southern Jurisdiction favors:

(1)   The American public school, non-partisan, nonsectarian, efficient, democratic, for all of the children of all the people.

(2)   The inculcation of patriotism, respect for law and order, and the underlying loyalty to the Constitution of the United States of America.

(3)   The compulsory use of English as the language of instruction in the grammar grades of our public schools.

(4)   Adequate provision in the American public schools for the education of the alien populations in the principles of American institutions and ideals of citizenship.

(5)   The entire separation of Church and State, and opposition to every attempt to appropriate public moneys–federal, state, or local–directly, or indirectly, for the support of sectarian or private institutions.

70. What are some of the principles of the A.A.S.R., Northern Jurisdiction?

Declaration of Principles of the A.A.S.R.—Northern Jurisdiction:

This Supreme Council affirms its unswerving loyalty to the fundamental purpose and principles of Freemasonry.

It understands that purpose to be the improvement and strengthening of the character of the individual man, and through the individual, of the community.

It believes that this purpose is to be obtained by laying a broad basis of principle upon which men of every race, country, sect, and opinion may unite, rather than by setting up a restricted platform upon which only those of certain races, creeds and opinions can assemble.

Believing that good and wise men can be trusted to act well and wisely, it considers it the duty of the Fraternity to impress upon its members the principles of personal righteousness and personal responsibility, to enlighten them as to those things which make for human welfare, and to inspire them with that feeling of charity, or well-wishing, toward all mankind which will move them to translate principle and conviction into action.

To that end, it teaches and stands for the worship of God, for truth and justice, liberty and enlightenment, fraternity and philanthropy.

It believes in principles rather than programs. Principles unite men; programs divide them. Men may agree on principle without agreeing upon their particular application to some specific problem.

Nothing can be more important than the preservation of the essential and permanent sympathy and unity of purpose of those who are unable to agree as to the wisest action under special and temporary conditions.

It is of the essence of Freemasonry that this unity be preserved.

Believing this, the Supreme Council affirms its continued adherence to that ancient and approved rule of Freemasonry which forbids the discussion within tyled doors of creeds, politics, or other topics apt to excite personal animosities.

It further affirms its conviction that it is not only contrary to the fundamental principles of Freemasonry, but exceedingly dangerous to its unity, strength, usefulness and welfare for Masonic Bodies in their official capacity to take formal action or attempt to exercise pressure or influence for or against any particular legislative project or proposal, or in any way attempt to procure election or appointment of government officials, whether executive, legislative or judicial, or to influence them, whether or not members of the Fraternity, in the performance of their official duties. The true Freemason should act in civil life according to his individual judgment and the dictates of his conscience.

(Pages 102 and 103 of the *Proceedings* of the Supreme Council 1934—Grand Rapids, Michigan)

71. Are the degrees and bodies in the Southern Jurisdiction arranged the same as in the Northern Jurisdiction of the Scottish Rite?

No. See the following listing:

Southern Jurisdiction	*Northern Jurisdiction*
Symbolic Lodges, 1-3	Symbolic Lodges, 1-3
Lodges of Perfection, 4-14	Lodges of Perfection, 4-14
Chapters of Rose Croix, 15-18	Councils of Princes, 15-16
Councils of Kadosh, 19-30	Chapters of Rose Croix, 17-18
Consistories, 31-32	Consistories, 19-32
Supreme Council, 33	Supreme Council, 33

PART XII

Other Masonic Fraternal Bodies and Research Lodges

1. There are many other Rites and Orders of Freemasonry in the United States in addition to those found in the Lodge, Chapter, Council, Commandery and Scottish Rite. What are some of them?

Red Cross of Constantine; Royal Order of Scotland, Allied Masonic Degrees; Holy Royal Arch Knight Templar Priests; Grand College of Rites; Knight Masons (Green Degrees); Masonic Order of the Bath; York Cross of Honour; Masonic Rosicrucian Society; Ye Antient Order of Corks; The Blue Friars; Philalethes Society; Operative Masonry and the Rite of Strict Observance (C.B.C.S.).

2. What are the qualifications necessary for membership in these various bodies?

Qualifications differ, but all are "invitation" bodies; they cannot be petitioned for.

3. How does one aspire for membership in such bodies?

By doing research work in Masonry, or some other outstanding Masonic work so that one becomes well known to those who control these groups.

4. What sort of Masonic work do these bodies perform?

Some confer knighthoods, such as the York Cross of Honour and the Masonic Order of the Bath. Some confer degrees, such as the Knight Masons, Red Cross of Constantine and Royal Order of Scotland. Others control degrees, but never confer them, such as The Grand College of Rites and the Allied Masonic Degrees. Others are honorary, such as The Blue Friars and the Philalethes Society.

5. There are some Masonic bodies chartered by Grand bodies whose function is not to confer degrees. What are they?

Research lodges and chapters, established for Masonic research only.

6. Name some of these.

The North Carolina Lodge of Research No. 666, A.F.& A.M., chartered February 10, 1931 was the first one in the U.S.A. (The Charter was revoked Dec. 3, 1954); The American Lodge of Research, F.& A.M. in New York, chartered May 7, 1931. There have been several others—in Connecticut, Washington, etc. Also, a Chapter of Research in Ohio.

7. How does one become a member of such bodies?

By petition.

8. What is the one qualification necessary to become a member of a Research lodge or chapter?

He must already be a member of a lodge or chapter and thus becomes a member by affiliation.

9. There are usually two classes of membership in the Research bodies—sometimes three. What are they?

Active members, who control the body and are elected in the usual manner, by ballot. Associate, or corresponding members, usually elected by show of hands. Fellows, elected by ballot for unusual or conspicuous Masonic service or distinction.

10. By what method are the discussions and papers, read at the Masonic Research bodies, distributed to the membership?

By printed *Proceedings* or *Transactions*.

11. What is the difference between *Proceedings*, *Transactions*, and *Annuals*?

They are names given the same thing.

12. Do Research lodges contribute the same per capita tax as other lodges?

That depends upon the law of the particular Grand Lodge which charters the Research body. Some require contributions while others consider the contribution made by the members in the regular lodge sufficient.

13. There are some independent Masonic organizations which are found in most Masonic jurisdictions which are not national. What are they?

Past Masters Associations; Council Officers Associations; Craftsmen's Clubs; Fellowcraft Clubs; High Twelve Clubs; Square Clubs; Low Twelve Clubs.

14. There is a national body connecting a group of similar bodies with each other. What is it called?

The National League of Masonic Clubs.

15. There is a national group composed of past or presently commissioned officers of our armed forces who are Masons. What is the name of this organization?

The National Sojourners.

16. There is a side degree connected with the National Sojourner. What is the name of this group?

Heroes of '76.

17. Is it necessary that the Master of a Research lodge have been a Past Master of a Symbolic lodge?

No, but when he becomes Master of the Research lodge it is necessary that the Past Master, or Qualifying Degree, be conferred on him if in a jurisdiction where this is required of all Masters. He is then a Past Master in such jurisdiction.

18. What function is usually found only in a Research lodge in the United States and not in ordinary lodges?

The "Tyler's Toast."

19. What is the "Tyler's Toast"?

Usually a song sung in memory of the absent and departed brethren.

20. Is the "Tyler's Toast" given in lodges in England?

Yes, and may be proposed by any brother at the wish of the Master. It is the final toast at the dinner before leaving.

21. Why is it called the "Tyler's Toast"?

It was observed in 1762, and possibly earlier, and was generally regarded as the Tyler's privilege.

22. What famous author wrote a Masonic poem in which the "Tyler's Toast" is the motif?

Kipling in *The Widow at Windsor*, referring to Queen Victoria. The paraphrase ends: "Then 'ere's to the sons o' the Widow, Wherever, 'owever they roam. 'Ere's all they desire, an' if they require, A speedy return to their 'ome. (Poor beggars!—they'll never see 'ome!)"

23. In 1928 a Masonic society, to be composed of Forty Fellows, and any number of members, was formed in St. Louis, Missouri. This Society is restricted to Masonic writers, editors and students. What is its name?

The Philalethes Society.

24. In 1932 another Masonic society was formed in North Carolina, limited to Masonic writers, one member to be elected each year. What is its name?

The Blue Friars.

25. How long have Past Masters associations been operating in American Masonry?

The first Association was formed on October 25, 1895, in Long Branch, New Jersey.

26. What is the York Cross of Honour?

An organization made up of Masons who have rendered service in York Rite Masonry, having been a Past Master, a Past High Priest, a Past Master of the council, and a Past Commander. It is called a Priory. The Order was founded in Monroe, North Carolina, on March 13, 1930.

27. What is the Grotto?

It is known as the Mystic Order of Veiled Prophets of the Enchanted Realm. It is not Masonic, but a qualification for membership is that one be a Master Mason. It is an organization for good fellowship and in some respects resembles the Shrine. The Grotto was organized in Hamilton, New York, on September 10, 1899. In 1951 there were about 215 active "Grottoes."

28. What are High Twelve Clubs?

Groups of Masons meeting for a luncheon period where a speaker is usually presented.

29. What are Low Twelve Clubs?

Clubs with insurance benefits, but they are Masonic only in membership. The Masonic fraternity has no insurance benefits.

30. What are the Tall Cedars of Lebanon?

A non-Masonic group composed of Master Masons, formed for good fellowhip. It was organized in Trenton, New Jersey, March 18, 1902. In 1950 there were 49 "Forests" in 10 eastern states.

31. What are the Sciots?

A good fellowship group of Master Masons. It was formed in San Francisco, California, in 1905, as "The Boosters" and in January, 1910 the name was changed to "Ancient Egyptian Order of Sciots." In 1951 there were about 20 "Pyramids" in California and Arizona.

32. What is the Shrine?

A group formed for social intercourse among Freemasons who are either Knights Templar or 32^0 Scottish Rite Masons. It was formed September 26, 1872, in New York City, and became a national body on June 6, 1876. Their great work is supporting hospitals for crippled children. In 1951 there were about 160 "Temples."

PART XIII

Black Freemasonry

1. In what year were blacks first made Freemasons in America?

March 6, 1778, in Boston, Massachusetts, when a John Batt 'conferred' the 'Marster' degree on two black men: Prince Hall and Thomas Sanderson. Also, the Entered Apprentice and Fellow Craft on Cyrus Forbes and Bristol Slensor. This was the start of Batt 'conferring' degrees on black men. The names of the 15 and dates they received degrees are recorded on a slip of paper, among which are the following 'Marsters': May 30, 1778 — 2; June 2, 1778 — 2 [one of these died June 20]; May 14, 1779 — 1; May 28, 1779 — 1; June 23, 1779 — 2; January 26, 1780 — 1; and four others without dates.

2. Who was John Batt?

An ex-British Army sergeant, having been discharged in Staten Island, N.Y. on Feb. 23, 1777, following 18 years service in the 38th English Regiment. Irish Lodge No. 441 was attached to this regiment. At the time of the above 'conferring' the regiment was in Newport, R.I. and N.Y.C. Hence, the 'conferring' was done by Batt as an individual without any Masonic authority.

3. Who was the most outstanding black man among those who were given degrees?

Prince Hall, a well-known black man who had worked for a Hall family in Boston for 21 years when they gave him his freedom on April 9, 1770. According to a statement Hall made during the year he died, he was born in 1735. Having worked for the Halls since 1749, he had been in the Colonies at least 58 years.

4. What made Prince Hall an outstanding man in Boston?

He was a leader of black men there and, with several others, sent a petition to the legislature of Massachusetts protesting against the kidnapping and sale into slavery of a number of blacks who had been taken by force from Boston in a sailing vessel.

5. Did that petition produce any results?

Yes. The men were returned to Boston from St. Bartholomews (F.W.I.) at the request of the Governor of Massachusetts, John Hancock, who appealed to the French Consul.

6. What became of the Military Lodge No. 441?

It was moved from Boston to New York and became one of the lodges which participated in the formation of the first white Grand Lodge in New York.

7. What effect did this have on the blacks who had been initiated in Lodge No. 441?

On June 30, 1784, according to a copy of a letter written by Hall to the Grand Lodge of England, requesting a Charter, he stated that Grand Master Rowe (Prov. Grand Master, 1768-1787) had given them a "Permet to walk on St. John's Day and to bury their dead." There was no right given to initiate other persons and there is no record that such was done.

8. Did Prince Hall and his black brethren petition the white Grand Lodge of Massachusetts for recognition?

It is believed that Hall submitted a petition to Joseph Warren, Prov. Grand Master (1769-1775 of Scotland), but before any action could be taken, Warren was killed at the Battle of Bunker Hill.

9. Did this group of black men ever obtain a charter for a lodge?

Yes. They, and some additional brethren, petitioned March 2, 1784 and received a charter from the Grand Lodge of England, dated September 29, 1784.

10. When was this charter received?

After many delays, the document reached Boston on April 29, 1787 in the care of a Captain Scott.

11. When and where did they first meet under the charter?

May 6, 1787 at the Golden Fleece Tavern on Water Street, Boston, but as there was no such building or tavern — simply a sign on the front of Hall's place of business advertising leather, hides and fleece, this must be classed among the fables written in a book by William H. Grimshaw, a black man whose book was titled *Official History of Freemasonry Among the Colored People of North America*, 1903.

12. What was the name of the lodge?

African Lodge No. 459.

13. Who was the Master?

Prince Hall. He is variously called Grand Master, Master and Worshipful, but he was just the Master of the Lodge.

14. When did Prince Hall die?

On December 4, 1807, according to newspapers printed in Boston at the time. His name and date of death carved on the back of a stone marking the grave of Sarah Richery (first wife of the five women Hall married) in Copp's Hill, Boston, shows Dec. 7th, 1807. Sarah Richery Hall had died 38 years before. There is no record of Hall's burial.

15. Was there a black Provincial Grand Lodge?

Statements that such a body was formed on June 24, 1791 have appeared in print. Diligent search shows no record of such a body being formed. The Grand Lodge of England states that there never was a Provincial Grand Lodge of black men.

16. On April 18, 1792, the Grand Lodge of England renumbered its lodges. African Lodge No. 459 received what number?

No. 370.

17. Who were the first two Masters of Lodge No. 459-370?

Prince Hall, the first, and Nero Prince, the second. There is no record of when or how Prince Hall became Master of the Lodge because there are no minutes extant after the Lodge charter was received. After his death, a black servant of Edward Tuckerman was elected Master. He had been made a member of the Lodge August 20, 1799. As soon as he took office minutes were kept for the minutes of December 28, 1807, lists his installation.

18. What other black lodges were formed in 1797?

African Lodge in Philadelphia and Hiram Lodge in Providence, R.I. on June 24th and 25th, respectively. Although it has been stated that they were daughter lodges of No. 459 in Boston, it has been proved that they were started independently.

19. In 1813 the two independent Grand Lodges of England showed 908 lodges. On March 2, 1814, the United Grand Lodge of England published a new list of lodges. In the uniting, 261 lodges were eliminated, including 37 in the United States. African Lodge No. 370 was one of those eliminated. Why, and what then happened to the African Lodge No. 370?

Like the other lodges chartered by the English Grand Lodges in the Colonies, Lodge No. 370 had failed to pay into the Charity Fund of the Grand Lodge of England.

20. What happened to the Philadelphia Lodge?

It, with Union Lodge No. 2, Laurel Lodge No. 5 and Phoenix Lodge No. 6, all of Philadelphia, held an assembly on December 27, 1815 and organized a grand body for the State of Pennsylvania.

21. What was the name of the black Grand Lodge of Pennsylvania?

First Independent African Grand Lodge of Pennsylvania. This was later changed to Prince Hall Grand Lodge F.& A.M. of Pennsylvania.

22. What was the name of the first black lodge in New York?

Boyer Lodge No. 1, New York City, circa 1812, sometimes called "African Lodge of New York."

23. Were other lodges chartered in New York State?

About fourteen years later, in 1826, Celestial No. 2, New York City, Rising Sun No. 3, Brooklyn, and Hiram No. 4, New York City, were chartered.

24. These four lodges organized the New York Grand Lodge on March 14, 1845. What was it called?

Boyer Grand Lodge, F.& A.M. which was changed in 1848 to United Grand Lodge, F.& A.M., and again on December 27, 1878 to Grand Lodge, F.& A.M. In 1919, the words "Prince Hall" were added. At the annual session in June, 1944, the name Prince Hall Grand Lodge, F.& A.M. of the State of New York was adopted.

25. What did black brethren do that the white brethren talked about, but never did?

Formed a National Grand Lodge in 1847.

26. Was the National Grand Lodge a success?

No, but a few of the lodges they chartered still exist but are not recognized by the Prince Hall bodies.

27. What was the purpose underlying the formation of the National Grand Lodge of North America?

To provide uniformity in the ritual and to suggest plans for the general betterment of the Prince Hall Craft, and to bring various State bodies into a closer relationship.

28. With such admirable purposes, why did the National body fail?

Some of the State bodies were dissatisfied with the general management which had sought to make national legislation mandatory upon the State grand bodies, the State bodies holding that there is no higher authority in the American Masonic system than the Grand Lodge erected in each of the various States.

29. Were these black lodges and Grand Lodges recognized by the white Freemasons in the United States?

No. The white Grand Lodges only recognize one Grand Lodge in each State.

30. What is the difference between the work done in the black lodges and white lodges?

None, as both came from the same place—the Grand Lodge of England.

31. Are there any white men in the black lodges?

Yes, from time to time, white brethren are found in Prince Hall lodges.

32. Have any Prince Hall Masons ever become members of a lodge recognized by the white Masons?

Yes, at least three members have been initiated, passed, and raised all over again in Alpha Lodge No. 116, F.& A.M., then black, of Newark, New Jersey.

33. Are there any black Masons in the white lodges?

Yes, there are records of several. Also, there is a black lodge under the white Grand Lodge of New Jersey. On May 8, 1975, a lodge of black men received a charter from the Grand Lodge of New York. It is largely composed of members from Alpha Lodge No. 116, New Jersey.

34. What is the name of the New Jersey lodge and where is it located?

Alpha Lodge No. 116, in Elizabeth.

35. When did Alpha Lodge No. 116 start working?

The Charter was granted January 19, 1871, but to white brethren who, during the second year of its existence, "raised" nine black men.

36. How many white brethren have been members of Alpha Lodge?

Nine charter members and ten others.

37. Are any white brethren now in membership in Alpha Lodge?

No, the last two were S.N.P.D. on November 14, 1929.

38. Who was the first black Master of Alpha Lodge, and when?

Abram T. Cooke, one of the first nine black members, who served as Master in 1879. Three others of the first nine were also Masters.

39. What famous black actor became a member of a white lodge in Scotland?

"Bert" Williams was raised June 1, 1904, in Waverly Lodge No. 597, Edinburgh.

40. Were there any other black men made Masons in the Edinburgh Lodge?

Yes, nine others, all members of the Williams and Walker Company, then playing in Scotland.

41. What white New York lodge, at the request of the Grand Lodge of Scotland, conducted the Masonic funeral over the remains of "Bert" Williams?

St. Cecile Lodge No. 568, on March 6, 1922, in the Masonic Temple, New York City.

42. Is black Freemasonry confined to the lodge?

No, there are chapters, councils, commanderies, and they have two Supreme Councils of the Scottish Rite.

43. How does the membership of black Masonry compare with that of white Masonry?

In 1948 the ratio was about one to ten, but this has narrowed considerably in recent years.

44. Are there any lodges, or Grand Lodges, not of Prince Hall affiliation among the colored men?

Yes, there are independent Grand Lodges not recognized by Prince Hall Masonry. Most of these came directly, or indirectly, from the National Grand Lodge and are slowly becoming absorbed by the Prince Hall groups.

45. Are there also androgynous bodies and "fun degrees?

Yes, the Eastern Star, Amaranth, Heroines of Jericho, Daughters of Isis, Daughters of the Sphinx, Cyrenes, Order of the Golden Circle, Shrine, etc.–are all part of the system today.

46. What is the present attitude of the white Freemasons toward the black Freemasons?

A sympathetic attitude and respect for the wonderful work and progress which the black Freemasons have accomplished among their people. From the time of William H. Upton, Past Grand Master of the white Grand Lodge of Washington, down through the years, leading white Freemasons have been lending assistance and counsel in a true spirit of brotherhood. Neither the black nor the white solicit inter-visitation, but each group recognizes that the spirit of Freemasonry belongs not to any one particular race, creed, or color.

119

PART XIV

Officers' Titles

1. What are the titles of Grand Lodge Officers?

Grand Master: *Most Worshipful;* all others are *Right Worshipful;* Masters and Past Masters: *Worshipful.* In Pennsylvania, the Grand Master is also *Right Worshipful.* In some Grand Jurisdictions some officers do not carry the title Right Worshipful, but the majority do. District Deputy Grand Masters and Grand Representatives: *Right Worshipful* (in most jurisdictions).

2. What are the titles of Grand Chapter Officers?

Grand High Priest: *Most Excellent;* all other officers: *Right Excellent;* High Priests and Past High Priests: *Most Excellent High Priest* or *Excellent High Priest,* according to the jurisdiction.

3. What are the titles of the Grand Council Officers?

Grand Master: *Most Illustrious* (sometimes: *Most Puissant);* all other officers: *Right Illustrious;* Masters and Past Masters: *Illustrious* (or *Illustrious Master,* or *Thrice Illustrious Master),* according to the jurisdiction.

4. What are the titles of the Grand Commandery Officers?

Grand Commander: *Right Eminent;* Deputy Grand Commander: *Very Eminent;* all other officers: *Eminent,* including the Commanders and Past Commanders.

5. What are the titles of the General Grand Chapter Officers?

General Grand High Priest: *Most Excellent;* other officers down through the General Grand Captain of the Host: *Right Excellent;* the rest: *Excellent.*

120

6. What are the titles of the General Grand Council Officers?

General Grand Master: *Most Puissant;* the others: *Right Puissant,* except the General Grand Sentinel who is *Puissant.*

7. What are the titles of the Grand Encampment Officers?

Grand Master: *Most Eminent;* all the rest: *Right Eminent.* The Constitution of this body states that the titles are honorary.

8. What are the titles of the Officers of the Supreme Council of the Scottish Rite?

Sovereign Grand Commander. Officers of the Supreme Council and Active Members all have the title *Illustrious.* This is also the title of the Honorary Members of the S.C. There continues to be a mis-title abounding called "Honorary 33°." No such title exists. Members who have the rank of *Sovereign Grand Inspector General* (33°) and are not Active Members are elected to Honorary Membership in the Supreme Council.

9. Who are the presiding officers in the Shrine, Grotto, and Tall Cedars?

Potentate, Monarch, Grand Tall Cedar, respectively.

10. By what names are the members designated in the following:

Symbolic Lodge	—Brethren
Chapter	—Companions
Council	—Companions
Commandery	—Sir Knights
Scottish Rite	—Sublime Princes
Shrine	—Nobles
Grotto	—Prophets
Tall Cedars	—Cedars

11. What Grand Lodge Officer in England has no counterpart in American Freemasonry?

The Pro-Grand Master, who is the "working" Grand Master; the Grand Master is, more or less, an honorary office.

PART XV

Awards and Honors

1. There are several special awards given by Grand Lodges to outstanding brethren in and out of their jurisdictions. Name that given by the Massachusetts Grand Lodge.

The Henry Price Medal, given for outstanding Masonic achievement.

2. What does the Grand Lodge of New York give?

The Medal for Distinguished Achievement.

3. What does the Grand Lodge of Maine give?

The Josiah Hayden Drummond Medal, given for outstanding proficiency in the knowledge of Freemasonry, and for distinguished service.

4. Name that of Nebraska.

The gold Jordan Medal, held by the oldest Freemason in Nebraska. There is also a bronze Jordan Medal, held by the oldest Freemason in each lodge in that State.

5. Name that of Connecticut.

The Pierpont Edwards Medal. Bronze, given for distinguished Masonic service, and silver given for eminent Masonic service.

6. Are there others?

Yes, The Jeremy L. Cross Medal and The John Sullivan Medal (N.H.); The Distinguished Service Medals (R.I. and D.C.); The Albert Gallatin Mackey Medal (S.C.); The Joseph Montfort Medal (N.C.); The Daniel Coxe Medal (N.J.) and The Philip C. Tucker Medal (Vt.).

7. Are there similar awards in other branches of Freemasonry?

Yes. The Scottish Rite has one, The Gourgas Medal; the Grand Chapter of Massachusetts has one; and some Grand Bodies (usually Knighthoods) have a Grand Cross awarded to distinguished members of their own bodies.

8. Was there ever a scholastic degree awarded in Freemasonry?

Yes, the Sovereign College of Allied Masonic Christian Degrees for America twice conferred such honors on distinguished members of that body. The dates were January 30, 1893 and January 25, 1894.

9. What were the names of these academic honors?

Doctor in Universal Masonry (5); Doctor in Masonic Law (3); Doctor in Masonic Letters (3); Doctor in Masonic Theology (5); Bachelor in Masonic Law (5). The numbers in parenthesis are the total conferred in each–21 in all.

10. Who were some of the prominent Freemasons who received any one of these degrees?

Dimetrius Rhodokonakis, of Greece; Earl of Euston, of London; William James Hughan, of England; D. Murray Lyon, of Scotland; Josiah Hayden Drummond, of the United States; George W. Warvelle, of the United States; Charles F. Matier, of England; Frederick Webber, of the United States.

11. What types of Masonic awards for length of membership are somewhat prevalent in the United States?

Twenty-five year buttons; fifty-year buttons or medals, with palms for sixty, seventy, and seventy-five years. Usually, if a brother reaches the eighty-year mark, a special medal is voted for him by Grand Lodge.

PART XVI

Interesting Facts
about a Few Interesting Freemasons

ADAMS, KENNETH S.

(1899-   ). Rose from warehouse clerk with Phillips Petroleum to Chairman of the Board. Bartlesville Lodge No. 284, Kansas; member of all bodies; 33⁰.

ALDRIN, JR., EDWIN EUGENE

(1930-   ). Better known as "Buzz." The first Freemason and one of the first two human beings to walk on another celestial body when he followed Neil Armstrong onto the lunar surface on July 20, 1969. Incidentally, his mother's maiden name was "Moon." Raised in Montclair Lodge No. 144, N.J. in 1956. Member of all bodies and received the 33⁰ (SJ).

ALEXANDER, GROVER C.

(1887-1950). A great National League pitcher. In 1926 he struck out Lazzeri with the bases full in the final inning, the Cardinals thus defeating the Yankees for the world championship. Raised in St. Paul Lodge No. 82, Neb., 1923.

ARMSTRONG, HARRY W.

(1879-1951). Famous for the all-time favorite *Sweet Adeline* which he wrote in 1903. Raised in Montgomery Lodge No. 68, N.Y.C., 1922.

ASHMOLE, ELIAS

(1617-1692). A learned antiquarian and archaeologist in England and founder of the famous Ashmolean Museum. His library was given to Oxford University. His diary records him as being made a Freemason on Oct. 16, 1646. The first Speculative Mason recorded.

ASTOR, JOHN JACOB

(1763-1848). A German-American financier who made his money in the fur trade and New York real estate. One of the very early members of Holland Lodge No. 8, N.Y., which he served as Master in 1788.

AU, DAVID W. K.

(?—?). The first Chinese ever to be elevated as Master of an English lodge (Royal Sussex No. 501, Shanghai) and instrumental in establishing the G.L. of China of which he was the first Grand Master in 1949.

AUTRY, GENE

(1908-   ). Started as a telegraph operator for the railroad and became our first cowboy singer, actor, writer and producer, as well as flight officer in WW2. Raised in Catoosa Lodge No. 185, Okla., 1927. 32⁰ and Shriner.

BAKER, BRYANT

(1881-1957). Sculptor who did many famous bronze statues in England as well as in the U.S. His heroic 17 foot bronze of George Washington at the Washington Masonic National Memorial in Alexandria, Va., was unveiled by Pres. Truman in 1950. Member of Constitutional Lodge No. 294, Beverly, Yorkshire, Eng.

BAKER, HOWARD H.

(1925-   ). Senator from Tenn. Selected as one of the seven-member select committee for the "Watergate" investigation. 32⁰ and Shriner.

BALCHEN, GERNT

(1899-   ). Came to the U.S. from his native Norway in 1926; naturalized in 1931. Became a Colonel in the U.S. Air Force. Piloted the first flight over the South Pole in 1929. He and Admiral Byrd dropped Masonic flags over both poles and Balchen dropped his Kismet Shrine fez over the South pole. Member of Norseman Lodge No. 878, N.Y., one of the organizers of the "Top of the World" Square Club at Thule, Greenland while helping to establish the air base there. Awarded the G.L. of N.Y. distinguished achievement medal in 1954.

BARNEWALL, GEORGE A.

(1888-1952). Vice-President of the old Brooklyn Dodgers baseball team. At the time of his death he was Dep. G.M. of the G.L. of N.Y. and had he lived a few weeks longer would have been install-ed as Grand Master. While a G.L. officer, Barnewall always arranged an afternoon "break" so the delegates could see his team play. Rais-ed in Continental Lodge No. 287, N.Y.

BARTHOLDI, FREDERIC A.

(1834-1904). Designer of our Statue of Liberty, which was a gift from the French people to those of the U.S. One of the early members of Lodge Alsace-Lorraine, Paris, 1875.

BEARD, DANIEL CARTER

(1850-1941). Known as "Dan." Organizer of the Boy Scout movement in the U.S. A painter and illustrator. Awarded the Golden Eagle by the B.S.A. Wrote many books on scouting. Raised in Mariners' Lodge No. 67, N.Y., 1917.

BEERY, WALLACE

(1889-1949). Started his famous movie career as a female im-personator. Ran away from home to join a circus and became an elephant trainer. Member of Blaney Lodge No. 271, Ill. 32° and Shriner.

BELLAMY, REV. FRANCIS

(1855-1931). Author of the American "Pledge of Allegiance" to the flag. Member of Little Falls Lodge No. 181, N.Y.

BELZONI, GIOVANNI BATTISTA

(1778-1823). Celebrated discoverer of Egyptian antiquities; opened the temple of Abu-Simbel and discovered the tomb of Seti I, Thebes, in 1817. Referred to as "Bro. Belzoni" when his widow was helped by the Lodge of Emulation (London) and Bedford Lodge No. 183 (E.C.).

BENDER, CHARLES A.

(1883-1954). Known as "Chief" in the baseball world. A Chippewa Indian who won over 200 games. Pitched for the Athletics in five World Series games. Raised in Robert A. Lamberton Lodge No. 487, Pa., 1911.

BENES, EDUARD

(1884-1948). President of Czechoslovakia in 1935. A disciple of Masaryk who worked for the Czech nationalist movement. Was re-elected President in 1945 when he returned from exile in England due to the German occupation of the Sudetenland. Was buried with both Catholic and Protestant services. Initiated in Jan Amos Komensky Lodge No. 1, Prague, and later passed and raised in Pravda Vitezi Lodge (Truth Shall Prevail), also of Prague, about 1927-28.

BENNETT, CHARLES R.

(-1855). His tombstone reads "Capt. Charles Bennett was discoverer of gold in California." Went to Calif. as a mule hostler with Gen. Fremont and while tending his mules at camp, picked up a small nugget which he recognized as gold. Later moved to Oregon and with gold he had mined, built the first hotel in Salem (located where the Masonic Temple now stands). He was a Captain of the Salem Oregon Mounted Rifles and while leading the company in the Yakima Indian War, was killed at Walla Walla. Masonic honors were given by Salem Lodge No. 4 at his burial. He was the first candidate to have been initiated in that lodge.

BENTON, THOMAS HART

(1816-1879). Civil War general who saved the valuable Masonic library of Confederate General Albert Pike by placing a guard of Federal troops around Pike's home in Little Rock. Raised in Iowa City Lodge No. 4, Iowa, 1849.

BERLIN, IRVING

(1888-   ). Composer of "God Bless America," "White Christmas" and hundreds of other top songs. Came from Russia when only five years old and his only education was two years in the N.Y.C. public schools. Served in WW1. Raised in Munn Lodge No. 190, N.Y., 1910. 32⁰ and Shriner.

BERNIE, BEN

(1893-1943). His real name was Abramovitz, but is known as the "Old Maestro." Started out to be an engineer, but switched to a violin salesman and then vaudeville. Served as master of ceremonies on many radio shows during his day. Member of Keystone Lodge No. 235, N.Y.

BOLIVAR, SIMON

(1783-1830). A Venezuelan statesman and general and is known as the "Liberator" of South American countries. Made a Mason in Cadiz, Spain; received the SR degrees in Paris and knighted in a Commandery of KT in France. Founded and served as Master of Protectora de las Vertudes Lodge No. 1, Venezuela and founded the Lodge Order and Liberty No. 2 in Peru. On his deathbed he returned to Catholicism, but it was as a Freemason that he performed the deed which established him as one of the greatest liberators of the world.

BONAPARTE, JOSEPH

(1768-1844). Eldest brother of Napoleon. Joseph was King of Naples in 1806-8 and of Spain in 1803-13. Was made a Mason at the Tuilleries in 1805 and in the same year was appointed as Grand Master of the Grand Orient of France by Napoleon. Following Napoleon's defeat, Joseph lived in Bordentown, N.J.

BONAPARTE, NAPOLEON

(1769-1821). It is claimed that he was made a Mason circa 1795. His four brothers (Jerome, Joseph, Louis and Lucien) were Freemasons. The Empress Josephine was initiated into adoptive Freemasonry in the Lodge Les Francs Chevaliers, at Paris, 1804.

BOOTH, GEN. BALLINGTON

(1859-1940). Commander-in-Chief of the Volunteers of America in 1896 after a disagreement with his father, Rev. Wm. Booth, founder of the Salvation Army, and brother of Evangeline C. Booth. Raised in Montclair Lodge No. 144, N.J. and later a member of Charter Oak Lodge No. 249, N.Y. Grand Chaplain of the G.L. of N.Y. Member of Kismet Temple.

BOOTH, EDWIN T.

(1833-1893). Famous Shakespearian actor. Made a Master Mason in New York Lodge No. 330, N.Y., Sept. 11, 1857.

BORGLUM, GUTZON

(1871-1941). Sculptor and painter and best known for the Mt. Rushmore national memorial in the Black Hills of S.D., but he did many other marbles and bronzes: Sheridan Equestrian (Wash. D.C.), marble head of Lincoln in the rotunda of the Capitol in Washington.

He designed and began carving the Confederate memorial on the face of Stone Mountain, Ga., but a controversy arose with the association and he destroyed all plans and models. He lived to see the fourth head of the Mt. Rushmore achievement, but not to complete the work which was finished by his son. Raised in Howard Lodge No. 35, N.Y.,1904. The cornerstone of his studio in Stamford, Conn. was laid with Masonic ceremonies for which special dispensation was obtained—it not being a public building.

BORGLUM, LINCOLN

(1912-   ). Sculptor and son of Gutzon. He completed Mt. Rushmore on which he had worked for 12 years in charge of measuring and enlarging models. Raised in Battle River Lodge No. 92, S.D.

BORGNINE, ERNEST

(1917-   ). Stage and screen actor who won an "Oscar" for the most honors given for a single performance in *Marty* in 1956. Served 10 years in the U.S. Navy and in WW2. Studied acting under the GI bill. He started on the legitimate stage with the Barter Theater in Va. and later played in N.Y. Played roles in *Hamlet* as well as the lead in *Born Yesterday* and *From Here to Eternity*. Member of Abingdon Lodge No. 48, Va. At one time was married to Ethel Merman.

BOSWELL, JAMES

(1740-1795). Famous biographer of Dr. Samuel Johnson. Boswell served as Dep. Grand Master of the G.L. of Scotland, 1776-78. Raised in Canongate-Kilwinning Lodge in 1759.

BRANT, JOSEPH

(1742-1807). Indian chief of the Mohawks. The first Indian Freemason of whom there is record. Probably raised in Hiram's Cliftonian Lodge No. 417, London. Was the first Master of Lodge No. 11, Brantford, Mohawk Village, Ontario, Canada.

BRYAN, WILLIAM JENNINGS

(1860-1925). Secretary of State under Woodrow Wilson and presidential nominee three times, being defeated twice by McKinley and once by Taft. He negotiated 30 treaties. Raised in Lincoln Lodge No. 19, Neb.

BURBANK, LUTHER

(1849-1926). The world-renowned plant scientist. Raised in Santa Rosa Lodge No. 57, Calif., 1921. 33⁰ in 1925.

BURNS, BOB

(1890-1956). Humorist and actor who gained his fame through homely philosophy in movies and radio. His famous homemade musical instrument, the "bazooka," was immortalized in WW2.

BYRD, JR., HARRY F.

(1914-   ). Governor and U.S. Senator from Va. who started with the *Winchester Star* newspaper at the age of 15 and now owns the paper as well as other publishing interests and the famous "Byrd Apple Orchards." Broke from the Democrats and became an Independent candidate and overwhelmingly endorsed by both Democrats and Republicans. Raised in Hiram Lodge No. 21, Va., 1925; received the 33⁰ in 1943.

BYRD, RICHARD

(1888-1957). Rear Admiral. Polar explorer and pioneer aviator. A brother of Harry F. Jr. Flew over the North Pole in 1926 with Floyd Bennett. Spent five months alone near the South Pole discovering new mountain ranges and islands. Member of Federal Lodge No. 1, Wash., D.C., 1921. He and his pilot, Bernt Balchen, *q.v.* dropped Masonic flags on the two Poles. In the Antarctic expedition of 1933-35, sixty of the eighty-two members were Freemasons and on Feb. 5, 1935, they established First Antarctic Lodge No. 777 of New Zealand constitution.

BYROM, JOHN

(1692-1763). English poet and inventor of an early shorthand system that was copyrighted in 1742. He was author of the phrase "tweedledum and tweedledee." Member of a lodge held at The Swan in Long Acre, England, 1750.

CALLAHAN, CHARLES H.

(1858-1944). He is credited with the idea that brought into being the George Washington National Masonic Memorial at Alexandria, Va. Member of Alexandria-Washington Lodge No. 22, Va. Grand Master of the G.L. from 1924-26.

CARSON, ENOCH TERRY

(1822-1899). An expert on Masonic documents and literature. He amassed a rare collection which is in the Library of the G.L. of Mass. Raised in Cynthia Lodge No. 155, Oh., 1846 and served as Master; also founder and first Master of Kilwinning Lodge No. 356, Oh. 33⁰.

CARSON, CHRISTOPHER "Kit"

(1809-1868). One of America's most famous plainsmen, Indian scout, guide, trapper and soldier. He was apprenticed to a saddler but ran away to join a party of hunters. His employer advertised in the *Missouri Intelligencer*, offering one cent reward for his return. Carson served as guide for Gen. John C. Fremont on the Calif. expedition. Probably best known white man among the western Indians. Raised in Montezuma Lodge No. 109, N.M. (then under Missouri charter).

CARTWRIGHT, ALEXANDER JOY

(1820-1892). Sometimes called the "father" of baseball because as a young lad in N.Y.C. he drew the diagram of a baseball diamond, set the rules of the game (9 men to a team), foul lines, batting order, 3 outs, etc. which are pretty much followed to the present time. Umpire Cartwright fined the pitcher for the N.Y. Nine 6¢ for swearing which was paid on the spot. He was made a Mason in Lodge Le Progress de l'Oceanie, Honolulu, 1850, which was chartered by the Sup. Council of France and later came under the G.L. of Calif. He later changed his membership to Hawaiian Lodge U.D. and served as Secretary and Master. He was acting Jr. G. Warden of the G.L. of Calif. when the first public Masonic ceremony was held in Hawaii, the laying of the cornerstone of the new Queen's Hospital. King Kamehameha IV, a P.M. of Lodge Le Progress acted as G.M.

CERNEAU, JOSEPH

(?—*circa*1840-45). A French jeweler who moved to the West Indies. The G.L. of Pa. granted a dispensation for a lodge in 1804 in Havana and Cerneau was named as Master. He was probably raised in a French Lodge. He received the SR 19⁰—25⁰ in Havana. He proceeded to set up a Sovereign Grand Consistory in N.Y.C. in 1807 for which he was expelled from his lodge and every degree in Masonry. The spurious Cerneau Supreme Council gained many members and it was only after several attempts by the legitimate S.C. at Charleston and decisions in the civil courts that it was declared clandestine and forced to abandon working. Cerneau returned to France where he died.

CERZA, ALPHONSE

(1905-   ). Lawyer. Born in Italy and came to the U.S. in 1916. Taught in a law school and is a famous book reviewer. Author and contributor of many articles for the M.S.A. and other organizations. Raised in Waubansia Lodge No. 160, Ill. which merged with other lodges. Master of Riverside Lodge No. 862, Ill. Grand Orator of the G.C.; 33⁰.

CHANDLER, ALBERT B. "Happy"

(1898-   ). Governor and State Senator of Ky. who was elected high commissioner of baseball in 1945 and served until 1951. Member of Landmark Lodge No. 41, Ky. M.M. in 1924. 32⁰ and Shriner.

CHENNAULT, MAJ. GEN. CLAIRE L.

(1890-1958). Famous for his "Flying Tigers" in WW2. Member of League City Lodge No. 1053, Texas; 32⁰ Orient of China; Islam Shrine, Calif.

CHURCHILL, SIR WINSTON L.

(1874-1965). British statesman and one of the most outstanding leaders of the 20th Century in both national and international levels. His mother was an American (Jeanette Jerome). Initiated in Studholme Lodge No. 1591, London and raised in Rosemary Lodge No. 2851, March 15, 1902.

CLAUDY, CARL H.

(1879-1957). One of the finest Masonic authors of the 19th Century whose interests and capabilities were varied. In 1898 he was a prospector and pioneer in Alaska; became director of publicity for National Highways Assoc.; editor of *American Inventor; Cathedral Calendar; The Master Mason;* aviation correspondent for *The New York Herald;* executive secretary of the Masonic Service Association. He wrote books not only on Masonry, but on photography, baseball, children, nature, men of Mars. Raised in Harmony Lodge No. 17, D.C.; Master, 1932; G.M., 1943. Member of all bodies; 33⁰.

CLAUSEN, HENRY C.

(1905-   ). Sov. Gr. Commander, Sup. Council 33⁰ (SJ) in 1969. Lawyer who was in charge of the investigation of the Pearl Harbor disaster of WW2 as Judge Advocate General's Dept. Member of Ingleside Lodge No. 630, Calif. and G.M. of the G.L. in 1954-55. Shriner.

CLAY, HENRY

(1777-1852). A leader in Masonry as well as in his country's affairs. Born in Va. but moved to Ky. Grand Master in 1820 and three times candidate for the presidency. Member of Lexington Lodge No. 1, Ky.

CLEMENS, SAMUEL LANGHORNE

(1835-1910). Better known as Mark Twain. An American author and humorist who was apprenticed to a printer at the age of 12. For a time he was a Mississippi River pilot before going west. He did mining and newspaper work, lectured and founded a publishing house which went broke. Member of Polar Star Lodge No. 79, Mo., 1861.

CLINTON, DE WITT

(1769-1828). Raised in Holland Lodge No. 8, N.Y. and served as Master in 1794. For 14 years he was G.M. of the G.L. Governor of N.Y. during the "Morgan Affair" and was the exponent of the Public School System for which the country will always revere him. He also served in the Grand Lodge, highest offices of the Grand Chapter, Gen. Grand Chapter and the state KT, as well as the first G.M. of the Grand Encampment.

COBB, TYRUS R. "Ty"

(1886-1961). One of the greats of baseball. Led the American League in batting 8 years in a row from 1908-15, and again, 1917-19 for Detroit. He retired with 419 major league hits with his all-time high batting average of .369. Member of Royston Lodge No. 426 (now 52), Ga. 32⁰ and Shriner.

CODY, WILLIAM F.

(1846-1917). Best known as "Buffalo Bill," the famous pony express rider, Indian fighter, scout, plainsman and showman. He contracted to supply buffalo meat to the laborers in the construction of the Kansas Pacific Railroad, thus earning the name "Buffalo Bill." During the Sioux outbreak in 1890-91, he was a general in the Neb. National Guard. From 1883 on he headed the famous "Wild West Show" that toured Europe, as well as America. Raised in Platte Valley Lodge No. 32, Neb., 1871; also a RAM, KT and AASR.

COHAN, GEORGE M.

(1878-1942). Famous theatrical actor, producer and song writer. A life member of Pacific Lodge No. 233, N.Y., in which he was raised in 1905. 32⁰ in 1906. His funeral was held in St. Patrick's Cathedral in N.Y.C.

COIL, HENRY WILSON

(1885-1974). Lawyer and author of *Outlines of Freemasonry, Comprehensive View of Freemasonry, Freemasonry through Six Centuries* and *Coil's Masonic Encyclopedia*. Raised in Las Animas Lodge No. 28, Colo. Master of Riverside Lodge No. 635, Calif.; member of all bodies, 33⁰ in 1957.

CROSS, JEREMY LADD

(1783-1860). An early American Masonic ritualist who introduced illustrations in the *Monitor* when his *The True Masonic Chart, or Hieroglyphic Monitor* was published in 1819. Raised in St. John's Lodge No. 1, N.H. Member of all bodies and 33⁰ (SJ).

d'ASSIGNY, FIFIELD

(1707-1744). A physician of Dublin, Ireland, who, in 1744, wrote *A Serious and Impartial Enquiry into the Cause of the Present Decay of Freemasonry in the Kingdom of Ireland.* The pamphlet is important because it is the first written reference to Royal Arch Masonry.

DAVIS, HARRY E.

A black Freemason who is author of the worthwhile book, *A History of Freemasonry among Negroes in America.*

DE GRASSE-TILLY, COUNT ALEXANDRE FRANCOIS AUGUSTE

(1776-1845). One of the two Catholics who were founders of the Mother Supreme Council AASR (SJ). The other was his son-in-law, J.B.N.M. Delahogue. His French fleet cooperated with Washington's army and made possible the victory at Yorktown. Member of the Lodge Contrat Social of Paris and, in 1796, became one of the founders and Master (1798) of Lodge La Candeur of Charleston, S.C. Became G.M. of the S.C. (Ancient) Grand Lodge in 1801.

DE KALB, BARON JOHANN

(1721-1780). Born in Germany, he was made a Major General in the Continental Army and served with valour in the cause of the Colonies. Mortally wounded in action on Aug. 16, 1780, he was buried with Masonic honors by Lord Cornwallis. Lafayette laid the cornerstone to a monument at Camden erected to De Kalb under auspices of Kershaw Lodge of S.C. It is not known where he received his Masonic degrees.

DE LAMATER, WALTER A.

(1880-1973). Maj. Gen. of the N.Y. National Guard. The 38th G.M. of the Grand Encampment, KT, 1955-58. Past Master of Kane Lodge No. 454, N.Y. Member of all bodies; 33° in 1947 (NJ).

DE MILLE, CECIL B.

(1881-1959). Motion picture producer who gave us some of the greatest spectacular movies ever produced. It is not generally known that he was organizer and president of the Mercury Aviation Co. (Calif.) in 1918-23 which was the first company to carry passengers on regular flights. Member of Prince of Orange Lodge No. 16, N.Y. Shriner (Calif.)

DEMOLAY, JACQUES

(1243?—1314). Grand Master of the early Templars on the Island of Malta. The King of France enticed him and other knights to come to France for the purpose of organizing an expedition to the Holy Land, but when they arrived, they were seized, their property confiscated and divided between the Pope and the King of France. DeMolay and others were burned at the stake. The Order of DeMolay for boys is named after this famous martyr.

DENSLOW, RAY VAUGHN

(1885-1960). Masonic author who started out in the photographic and newspaper business. He served as Grand Secretary and Recorder of the Grand Chapter, Grand Council and Grand Commandery of Missouri; Past Grand High Priest of the Gen. G. C.; 33⁰. Chairman of the foreign relief committee of the M.S.A. Raised in Twilight Lodge No. 114, Macon, Mo., 1906; G.M., 1931.

DEPEW, CHAUNCEY M.

(1834-1928). Famous orator. U.S. Senator from N.Y. Was appointed U.S. minister to Japan but declined and also declined appointment as Secretary of State under Pres. Harrison. Member of Courtland Lodge No. 34, N.Y., 1861. 33⁰.

DERMOTT, LAURENCE

(1720-1791). Born in Dublin and made a Mason there in Lodge No. 26, 1740. Grand Secretary of the Antient G.L. in England and active leader in the G.L. established in defiance of the premier G.L. He stopped the alteration of the ritual and invented the traveling warrants by means of which Freemasonry spread around the world wherever the army moved.

DESAGULIERS, DR. JOHN T.

(1683-1744). Mackey credits Desaguliers as being the "father of modern Speculative Freemasonry." He was born in France but with his family fled to England to escape the slaughter of Protestants when the Edict of Nantes was revoked. His reputation as a philosopher brought him a fellowship in the Royal Society. He was the inventor of heating by steam for various manufacturing purposes. A contemporary and friend of Sir Isaac Newton. Desaguliers was the 3rd G.M. of the G.L. of England (1719), but was in reality the first to exercise his prerogatives inasmuch as Anthony Sayer and George Payne, first and second Grand Masters, respectively, had done little more than have the title. While Anderson published the first *Constitutions*, Desaguliers was no doubt the planner and compiler of the work.

DEWEY, THOMAS E.

(1902-1971). Governor of N.Y. for three terms (1942, 1946 and 1950) and twice Republican nominee for President of the U.S. Gained recognition for his accomplishments as Special Prosecutor of Investigation of Organized Crime in N.Y. ("Murder, Inc."). Member of Kane Lodge No. 454, N.Y.; 33⁰ in 1948. Member of Kismet Shrine.

DOOLITTLE, MAJ. GEN. JAMES R.

(1896-1958). Led the first bombing force on Japan in 1942; active in North Africa Air Force; won honors as a speed pilot. Raised in Hollenbock Lodge No. 319, Calif., 1918. 33⁰ in 1945.

DOUGLAS, STEPHEN A.

(1813-1861). Gained fame by his debates with Lincoln who defeated him, but Douglas was a loyal supporter of the Lincoln administration. Raised in Springfield Lodge No. 4, Ill., 1840; Grand Orator of the G.L. of Ill. Member of the RAM.

DOVE, JOHN

(1792-1876). The first Virginian to write an extensive account of the Fraternity in the Old Dominion. Grand Sec'y of the G.L. from 1835 to 1876 and is the author of *The Virginia Text Book* which has gone into many editions and is still being used. Raised in St. John's Lodge No. 36, Va.

DOYLE, SIR ARTHUR CONAN

(1859-1930). English physician and author who created the characters of Sherlock Holmes and Dr. Watson. Raised in Phoenix Lodge No. 257, Portsmouth, England, 1887.

DRUMMOND, JOSIAH HAYDEN

(1827-1902). Lawyer, politician and Masonic writer. His *Historical and Bibliographical Memorandum* (1892) is one of the most sought for volumes by research students as he lists early books, magazines, Proceedings, etc. with dates, not found in other American bibliography of Masonic books. He served as presiding officer in all Grand Bodies in his native Maine, as well as of General Grand Chapter, Gen. Grand Council, and was Grand Commander of AASR (NJ) from 1867-1879. Raised in Waterville Lodge No. 33, Maine, 1849.

DUNCKERLEY, THOMAS

(1724-1795). A leader in propagating Royal Arch Masonry. On his mother's death he learned that he was the natural son of King George II and was given royal acknowledgment by way of a pension. At the age of 10 he ran away to sea and served with distinction in the Royal Navy for 36 years. Initiated at Three Tuns Lodge No. 31, Portsmouth, England, 1754. He held lodge on several ships on which he was serving and was responsible for the formation of several lodges in England.

EDWARD VIII (Duke of Windsor)

(1894-1972). King of England from Jan. 20 to Dec. 11, 1936 when he abdicated to marry Mrs. Wallis Simpson, an American. The first bachelor king in 176 years. Initiated in Household Brigade Lodge No. 2614, 1919. 33°.

ELLINGTON, EDWARD K. "Duke"

(1899-1974). Famous black jazz pianist and band leader, as well as composer. Initiated in Social Lodge No. 1, Prince Hall, Wash., D.C., 1932.

ERVIN, JR., SAMUEL J.

(1896-   ). Justice of the Sup. Court of N.C. Congressman and chairman of the congressional investigating committee on "Watergate." Wounded twice in WW1.Raised in Catawba Valley Lodge No. 217, N.C. 32º.

FAIRBANKS, SR., DOUGLAS

(1883-1939). Famous movie star of the silent films. His third marriage was to Mary Pickford. Raised in Beverly Hills Lodge No. 528, 1925. About a thousand Masons attended that meeting, among them were Harold Lloyd, Douglas McLean, James Neil, Milton Sills, Herbert Rawlinson, Chester Conklin, Fred Warner, Tom Mix, Duke Lee, Roy Stewart and 57 employees of Fairbanks' studio.

FIELDS, WILLIAM C.

(1880-1946). Motion picture and stage comedian. Famous for his bulbous nose and "Fieldisms" such as "never give a sucker an even break," "my little chickadee," etc. Member of C. Coppee Mitchel Lodge No. 602, Pa.

FINDEL, GOTTFRIED JOSEPH G.

(1828-1905). German Masonic writer who wrote the first comprehensive history of Freemasonry which was translated into English and published 1865-9. This was the forerunner of Gould's later work. Findel was initiated in Lodge Eleusis zur Vershwiegenheit, Bayreuth, 1856. In 1860, the Prince Hall Grand Lodge (black) of Mass. made him an honorary P.G.M. and named him representative of the P.H. groups in Germany.

140

FISHER, RT. REV. DR. GEOFFREY F.

(1887-   ). Archbishop of Canterbury. Known for his tolerance and unconventionality. Initiated in Old Reptonian Lodge No. 3725 in 1916. Grand Chaplain, 1937.

FLEMING, SIR ALEXANDER

(1881-1955). British discoverer of penicillin, 1928. Served as a private in the Scottish Rifles Regiment of London for 14 years in which he took special pride. A member of several English lodges and Master of Misericordia Lodge No. 3286 in 1935, as well as Master of Santa Maria Lodge No. 2682, 1925. RAM and SR member.

FLORENCE, WILLIAM JERMYN

(1831-1891). His real name was Bernard Conlin. An American actor who is recognized as the founder of the AAONMS along with Dr. Walter M. Fleming to whom Florence conveyed his ideas of the Shrine received while on one of his trips in North Africa. Received all three degrees by special dispensation in Mt. Moriah Lodge No. 155, Philadelphia, Pa. in 1853. Member of the RAM, KT and AASR; 33º. He was buried in a Protestant cemetery with Catholic rites arranged by his wife.

FORD, HENRY

(1863-1947). An innovative genius who helped change the transportation methods of the world. Noted for the "tin Lizzie" as well as for his philanthropy. Raised in Palestine Lodge No. 357, Detroit, Mich. in 1894 and remained a staunch member for almost 53 years. Received the 33º in 1940. He instituted a profit-sharing plan involving the distribution of many millions of dollars annually to employees in 1914, which was then unprecedented. His only son, Edsel, was not a Mason, but two of his grandsons (Benson and William C.) were raised in Corinthian Lodge No. 241, Detroit, at the same time in 1950. His third grandson and namesake, Henry II, became a Roman Catholic.

FRANKLIN, BENJAMIN

(1706-1790). Raised in St. John's Lodge, Philadelphia, in 1731 and served as G.M. of the G.L. in 1734, the same year he reprinted Anderson's *Book of Constitutions* of 1723. Invented many things, among which was a heating stove in 1744, which is still being manufactured and used today. He was recognized as the foremost scientist of the day not only in the U.S.A., but abroad. He did more for Masonry in this country than any other individual during his lifetime. In 1778, he assisted at the initiation of Voltaire in the Lodge of the Nine Sisters, Paris, France.

GARIBALDI, GIUSEPPE

(1807-1882). Italian liberator and known as the "George Washington" of Italy. He was condemned to death as a revolutionist and escaped to South America. Became a member of the Lodge Les Amis de Patrie of Montevideo, Uruguay, circa 1844. Later, when he came to the U.S., he affiliated with Tompkins Lodge No. 471, N.Y. He was Grand Master of the G.L. at Palermo in 1860 and became Grand Commander of the Supreme Council of the SR in Italy in 1863.

GIBBON, EDWARD

(1737-1794). English historian and author of *The Decline and Fall of the Roman Empire*, on which he spent 16 years of work. At an early age he was a Roman Catholic, but left the church. He received his degrees in the Lodge of Friendship No. 6, London. His close friend and fellow member of Parliament, Rowland Holt, and Thomas Dunckerley proposed Gibbon for the Royal Arch degree.

GODFREY, ARTHUR

(1903-   ). Famous radio and TV personality. Raised in Acacia Lodge No. 18, D.C., 1937. Member of the AASR and Almas Shrine.

GOETHE, JOHANN WOLFGANG VON

(1749-1832). German poet and the dominating influence of his era on the development of German literature. Wrote *Faust* and a Masonic novel, *Wilhelm Meister,* which is one of the finest stories given to the Fraternity; also was author of a poem, "A Mason's Ways." Raised in Lodge Amalia in Weimar, 1782.

GOLDWATER, BARRY M.

(1909-   ). U.S. Senator from Arizona. Unsuccessful presidential candidate in 1964. Noted as a "conservative." Pilot in the Air Force in WW2 from 1941-45. Raised in Arizona Lodge No. 2, 1932; member of AASR (SJ) and received the 33⁰ in 1959. Shriner.

GOMPERS, SAMUEL

(1850-1924). First president of the American Federation of Labor. Member of Dawson Lodge No. 16, D.C., 1904 and in 1924 a lodge was named for him, Samuel Gompers Lodge No. 45, D.C. In his autobiography, he said "In my Masonic life I have visited lodges in many lands, and I have learned that Freemasonry in many countries, particularly in Latin countries, is the principal means whereby freedom of conscience, of thought, and expression is preserved." 32⁰.

GOSDEN, FREEMAN F.

(1899-   ). "Amos" of the Amos and Andy radio show. In 1925 he, with Charles J. Correll, started their famous comedy team over WGN in Chicago as the Sam 'n Henry radio program which two years later became the long running Amos and Andy program. Raised in Petersburg Lodge No. 15, Va., 1922.

GOULD, ROBERT FREKE

(1836-1915). Author of many Masonic books, the most outstanding being his *History of Freemasonry.* Made a Mason in Royal Navy Lodge No. 429, Ramsgate, England; Sr. Gr. Deacon of the G.L.; a founder of Quatuor Coronati Lodge No. 2076.

GRIMSHAW, WILLIAM H.

A black Freemason who wrote *Official History of Freemasonry Among the Colored People of North America,* and which was published in 1903. The U.S. Pension Bureau gives the information that Grimshaw was a "doorkeeper in the main reading room of the Library of Congress from Oct. 1, 1897 to Oct. 20, 1924." While there is no proof as yet, it is believed that this book may have been the work of one Richard H. Gleaves, National Grand Master of the National Compact G.L. The book contains many errors but because of its title labeled "Official" it has been taken into account as fact by many through the years.

GRISSOM, VIRGIL E.

(1926-1967). Astronaut who lost his life in the Apollo spacecraft during ground testing with Edward H. White II and Lt. Comdr. Roger B. Chaffee. Raised in Mitchell Lodge No. 228, Ind. in 1949 while a student at Purdue University. Also a member of the RAM, KT, SR and Shrine. He was a life sponsor of the Knights Templar Eye Foundation, Inc.

GUEST, EDGAR A.

(1881-1959). Famous American poet who was born in Birmingham, England but came to the U.S. in 1891. Was connected with the Detroit Free Press for many years and it is said he wrote a poem a day. Raised in Ashlar Lodge No. 91, Mich. and member of the RAM, KT, AASR and Shrine. 33° given him in 1921.

GUILLOTIN, DR. JOSEPH IGNACE

(1738-1814). A French Freemason. Although the guillotin used for executions was named after him, it is neither true that he invented it nor met his death by it, as often stated. He was a physician and a deputy to the French Assembly and urged capital punishment be inflicted as speedily and painlessly as possible and argued for a machine to accomplish this. The machine was first used April 25, 1792 for the execution of a highwayman named Oelletier. Guillotin was Master of Concorde Fraternelle Lodge in Paris and also a member of the famous Lodge of the Nine Sisters. In 1778, he was founder of the society which became the Academy of Medicine.

144

GUSTAVUS V

(1858-1950). King of Sweden who played tennis well past his 80th birthday and his favorite hobby was knitting altar pieces for churches. Made a Mason on Jan. 13, 1877 and served as G.M. until his death. He took an active part in Masonic work all his life.

HAHN, CONRAD

(1906-1977). Executive Secretary of the M.S.A. since 1964 until his death on Dec. 15. Past Master of Apollo Lodge No. 59, Conn.; Grand Master, 1957. 33⁰ (NJ). Received highest awards from many Grand Lodges for his achievements and furtherance of Masonic education.

HALL, MANLY PALMER

(1901-   ). Author and lecturer; founder of The Philosophical Research Society, Inc. of Calif., an educational corporation devoted to the study of comparative religion, idealistic philosophy and analytical psychology. Raised in Jewel Lodge No. 374, Calif., in 1954; 33⁰.

HALL, PRINCE

(1748-1807). Father of black Freemasonry in the U.S. Many black Grand Lodges are named for him.

HANCOCK, JOHN

(1737-1793). First signer of the Declaration of Independence. When asked why he wrote his name so boldly he replied "so that George III may read it without putting on his glasses." Elected the first governor of the Commonwealth of Mass. and served 9 terms until his death in 1793. Made a Mason while traveling in Quebec in Merchant's Lodge No. 1, in 1762. He later affiliated with St. Andrew's Lodge in Boston.

HANDY, WILLIAM C.

(1873-1958). American black composer known as "Father of the Blues." Member of Prince Hall bodies, including the 33⁰.

HARDY, OLIVER

(1892-1957). Comedian of stage and screen. Half of the "Laurel and Hardy" team. Member of Solomon Lodge No. 20, Fla. and a frequent visitor at Hollywood lodges.

HAYDN, FRANZ JOSEPH

(1732-1809). Austrian composer regarded as the first great master of the symphony and the quartet. He had a long friendship with Mozart who was present on the occasion of Haydn's receiving his E.A. degree in the lodge Zur Wahrn Eintracht, Vienna, in 1785.

HAYS, WILL H.

(1879-1954). Postmaster General of the U.S., but perhaps better remembered as the "czar" of the motion picture industry from 1922-45 during the "censoring" period. Raised in Sullivan Lodge No. 263, Ind., 1900 and given the 33⁰ in 1945.

HAYWOOD, HARRY LE ROY

(1886-1956). Masonic author, having written some 20 books on Freemasonry. Raised in Acacia Lodge No. 176, Iowa, 1915. Affiliated with Waterloo No. 105, Iowa, Publicity Lodge No. 1000, N.Y. and Mizpah Lodge No. 639, Iowa. Ordained a minister at 18 but gave up preaching and taught and lectured on religion and anthropology for 13 years in many major colleges of the U.S. Editor of *The Builder*, official journal of the Nat'l Mas. Research Society and the *New York Masonic Outlook*. Considered the dean of Masonic historians and writers of his generation. Member of the RAM and 32⁰.

HINES, EDWARD N.

(1870-1938). Designed and built the first mile of concrete road in the U.S. Originated the white line separating traffic lanes. Member of Ashlar Lodge No. 91, Mich., 1893.

HOBAN, JAMES

(1762?-1831). Architect who designed and supervised the construction of the White House. He was a devout Catholic. Under his leadership, a group of Irish Catholics and Scotch Presbyterians organized Federal Lodge No. 1, D.C., and he was the first Master.

HOGARTH, WILLIAM

(1697-1764). English painter famous for his caricature and satirical paintings. An active Mason; Gr. Steward of the G.L. of England, 1735; member of the lodge at "Ear and Harrow." Best known Masonically for his Masonic engraving called "Night."

HOOPER, DEWOLF

(1858-1935). Comedian noted for his recitation of "Casey at the Bat." Raised in Pacific Lodge No. 233, N.Y., 1890. 32⁰ and Shriner.

HOOVER, J. EDGAR

(1895-1972). Director of the F.B.I. for many years. Made a Mason in Federal Lodge No. 1, D.C., on Nov. 9, 1920 and affiliated with Justice Lodge No. 46 as a charter member in 1926. Member of all bodies; 33⁰ on Oct. 21, 1955.

HORNSBY, ROGERS

(1896-1963). One of the original members of the Baseball Hall of Fame. With both National and American Leagues. Nat'l League batting champion for 7 years, 1920-25 and 1928. Managed the Cardinals to the World Championship in 1926. Raised in Beacon Lodge No. 3, St. Louis, 1918; RAM and KT.

HOUDINI, HARRY

(1874-1926). Famous magician and escape artist who was the son of Rabbi Mayer S. Weiss. He took his stage name from the great French prestidigitator, Robert Houdini, and had it legalized. Member of St. Cecile Lodge No. 568, N.Y., 1923; Mecca Shrine, N.Y.

HOUDON, JEAN ANTOINE

(1740-1828). French sculptor. His famous statue of Washington stands in the rotunda of the Capitol in Richmond, Va. Member of Nine Sisters Lodge, Paris. His name appears in its list of members in 1779, 1783, 1784 and 1806.

HOUSTON, GEN. SAM

(1793-1863). Under his leadership, the Mexicans were defeated at the Battle of San Jacinto and thus the Republic of Texas was born of which he was the first president. A native Virginian, but when his father died the family moved to Tenn. and he spent his early years with the Indians and was adopted by one of them. Received his degrees in Cumberland Lodge No. 8, Nashville, Tenn., 1817. The proceedings of 1828 (page 236) list him as suspended for unMasonic conduct! He affiliated with Holland Lodge No. 36 of La. in 1837 and this became Holland Lodge No. 1 of Texas. He presided over the meeting which established the G.L. of Texas.

HUGHAN, WILLIAM JAMES

(1841-1911). Made a Mason in St. Aubyn Lodge No. 954, Devonport, England in 1863. One of the greatest Masonic research students and writers. Author of many books, the most outstanding of which is *The Origin of the English Rite.* Collaborated with Gould on Gould's *History* and was also a founder of Quatuor Coronati Lodge No. 2076, London.

HUTCHINSON, WILLIAM

(1732-1814). An 18th Century English literary scholar who wrote *The Spirit of Masonry* in 1774, which did much to elevate the spirit and character of the Craft. Master of Lodge of Concord in Barnard Castle.

JONES, JOHN PAUL

(1747-1792). Often called the "Father of the American Navy." His body rests in the crypt of the Chapel of the U.S. Naval Academy, Annapolis, Md., placed there Jan. 26, 1913. He was born in Scotland and made a Mason in 1770 in St. Bernard's Lodge No. 122, Kirkcudbright. He died in France and was buried in a Protestant cemetery and his graveside was forgotten until 1905 when it was rediscovered and the remains shipped to Annapolis.

JUAREZ, BENITO PABLO

(1806-1872). Mexican patriot and president whose parents were pure Indian. Led the successful revolution against Maximilian, Archduke of Austria, who had been sent to Mexico by Napoleon III to set up a monarchy. Juarez was as active in Masonry as he was in politics and rose in the councils of the Craft until he became Sov. Inspector General of the Mexican National Rite; 33⁰.

KALAKAUA, KING DAVID

(1836-1891). King of Hawaii, 1874-91. Raised in Lodge Le Progress de l'Oceanie No. 124 in 1859 (now No. 371 on G.L. of Calif. Register). Member of the RAM, KT and received the 33⁰ in 1878.

KAMEHAMEHA IV, KING

(1834-1863). King of Hawaii, 1854-63. His name was Alexander Liholiho. He was the nephew of Kamehameha III. He introduced the use of the English language in Hawaiian schools. Raised in Lodge Le Progress de l'Oceanie No. 124 (later No. 371 under Calif.). Served as Master for three years. A crowning act of his reign, and a monument to him, was the founding of the Queen's Hospital for which he laid the cornerstone with Masonic ceremonies in 1860.

KAMEHAMEHA V, KING

(1830-72). Older brother of Kamehameha IV. King of Hawaii, 1863-72. The first Hawaiian to be made a Freemason. Last of a direct line of Sandwich Island kings. During his reign the Molokai Leper Settlement was established (1864). Raised in Hawaiian Lodge No. 21 (Calif.) in 1854. At that time he was Prince Lot Kamehameha.

KING, ADMIRAL ERNEST J.

(1878-1956). Commander-in-Chief of the U.S. Fleet, 1941 at the time of the "Pearl Harbor" invasion. Raised in George C. Whiting Lodge No. 22, D.C., 1935. Member of the RAM, KT and Al Koran Shrine.

KIPLING, RUDYARD

(1865-1936). Born in Bombay, India. Made a Mason in Hope and Perseverance Lodge No. 782 (E.C.), Lahor, India in 1886. He said he was "entered by a Hindu, passed by a Mohammedan, and raised by an Englishman." This statement was allegory but has been taken as fact for many years. The minutes of the Lodge are extant and show that a Christian Freemason presided in each of the three degrees. The truth is that Kipling acted as secretary of the Lodge and wrote the minutes!

KNUDSEN, WILLIAM S.

(1879-1948). President of General Motors, 1937-48. In charge of production for the War Dept. for WW2. He served as a bicycle mechanic in Denmark and came to the U.S. when only 20 years old where he first worked in shipyards. Raised in Palestine Lodge No. 357, Mich. Received the 33^0 (NJ) in 1943.

KOMATSU, TAKASHI

(1886-   ). The first native-born Japanese to become Master of a Masonic lodge (Tokyo No. 125), under Philippine constitution, 1955. A Japanese executive connected with shipbuilding and steel. 32^0 and Shriner.

KOSSUTH, LAJOS (Louis)

(1802-1894). Hungarian statesman and patriot who fought for the independence of Hungary from Austria. When this failed, he fled to Turkey, Italy and, finally, the U.S. Raised in Cincinnati Lodge No. 133, Ohio, in 1852, during his stay in the U.S. He later returned to Italy where he gave valiant service to the Italian liberators, Massini and Garibaldi. Also a member of Cincinnati Chapter No. 2, RAM.

LAFAYETTE, MARQUIS DE

(1757-1834). Hero of the American Revolution in which he served without pay. Commissioned a Major General in the Continental Army and became one of Washington's closest associates. It has never been established where he was made a Mason, but there are many records in the U.S. and France of Masonic memberships. Member of the Royal Arch, 1824, KT and SR, including the 33⁰ in N.Y. He laid the cornerstone of the Bunker Hill Monument in Boston, 1825.

LAND, FRANK S.

(1890-1959). Founder of the Order of DeMolay (1919). When only 10 years old, he conducted a Sunday School class of 300 and was known as the "Boy Preacher." Raised in Ivanhoe Lodge No. 446, Mo. and a member of all bodies including the 33⁰. Imperial Potentate of the Shrine, 1954-55.

LEE, HENRY "Light Horse Harry"

(1756-1818). Governor of Va. Washington appointed him a general in 1794 and gave him 15,000 troops to break up the "whiskey rebellion." He is credited with coining the phrase "First in war, first in peace and first in the hearts of his countrymen." Member of Hiram Lodge No. 59, Va., but it is believed that he was made a Mason in the Tappahannock (Hobbs Hole) Lodge. Father of Robert E. Lee who was not a Mason.

LEWIS, JOHN LLEWELLYN

(1880-1969). President of the United Mine Workers Association for many years and a strong union organizer. Raised in Good Shepherd Lodge No. 414, Iowa, 1902.

LINDBERGH, COL. CHARLES A.

(1902-1974). Known as the "Lone Eagle." His solo flight in "The Spirit of St. Louis" from N.Y. to Paris on May 20, 1927, arriving the next day after 33½ hours, made him the best known person of the day.

On this history-making flight, he wore the square and compasses on his jacket and his plane also bore a Masonic tag from his lodge. Raised in Keystone Lodge No. 243, Mo., 1926. He died at his home on the Island of Maui of cancer.

LIPTON, SIR THOMAS J.

(1850-1931). Born in Glasgow, Scotland where he opened a grocery store which expanded into a large chain of stores, dealing in tea, coffee, etc. An international sportsman who competed five times for the American Cup in yachting. Raised in Lodge Scotia No. 178, Glasgow in 1870 and at the time of his death was the oldest member of the Lodge.

LLOYD, HAROLD C.

(1894-1971). Movie star and producer who won world fame with his comedies with the Hal E. Roach studios. His large horned rimmed glasses without lenses and a straw hat were his "trademark." Raised in Alexander Hamilton Lodge No. 535, Calif., 1925. RAM; director of the Shrine Hospital for Crippled Children. Imperial Potentate for N.A. in 1949.

MAC ARTHUR, GEN. DOUGLAS

(1880-1964). Made a Mason "at sight" in 1936 by the G.M. of the Philippine Islands; affiliated with Manila Lodge No. 1. It could be reasonably stated that Gen. MacArthur was the greatest combat general the world has ever seen. Received the 33⁰ in 1947.

MACKEY, ALBERT GALLATIN

(1807-1881). Made a Mason in St. Andrews Lodge No. 10, Charleston, S.C. in 1841. He was a physician as well as America's most outstanding Masonic historian of his day. The first American to compile a book on Masonic jurisprudence and his books remain standard reference works. He held many Masonic offices in all bodies.

MAC MILLAN, DONALD BAXTER

(1874-1970). Arctic explorer and last survivor of the Peary Expedition of 1808-09. Member of Freeport Lodge No. 23, Maine. RAM, KT and Shriner.

MACOY, ROBERT

(1816-1895). Masonic author and publisher. Friend and contemporary of Rob Morris and when the latter went to the Holy Land he turned over his material on the Adoptive Rite to Macoy. Robert Macoy founded the "chapter system" of the Eastern Star and it is from his ritual that all Eastern Star rituals today are taken. His first Masonic book was the *Master Workman* which was published in 1849, the beginning of a Masonic publishing house which today bears his name and is known as the Macoy Publishing & Masonic Supply Co., Inc. Macoy was born in Ireland and died in NYC. Raised in Lebanon Lodge No. 13 (now No. 191), N.Y. He served as Grand Recorder of the Gr. Commandery KT of N.Y. for 44 years.

MARKHAM, EDWIN

(1852-1940). American poet. His *Man with the Hoe*, written in 1899, received world-wide recognition. Raised in Acacia Lodge No. 92, Calif. and later affiliated with El Dorado Lodge No. 26, Calif. The G.L. of Oregon nominated him for "poet laureate" of American Freemasonry and in 1935 the G.L. of N.Y. awarded him the N.Y. Grand Lodge Medal.

MARSHALL, FRANK A.

(1865-1931). Author of the DeMolay ritual. Journalist whose *Little Lay Sermons* were published on Sunday for many years in the *Kansas City Journal*. Raised in Westport Lodge No. 340, Ks. and a member of Chapter, Commandery, Council and received the KCCH in the SR in 1921.

MARSHALL, JOHN

(1755-1835). Chief Justice of the Supreme Court of the U.S. from 1801 until his death. His greatest service to the nation was to make the Supreme Court the place of last resort in determining the constitutionality of both federal and state laws. Member of Richmond Lodge No. 10 and Richmond-Randolph Lodge No. 19, both of Richmond, Va. Served two terms as Grand Master of the G.L. of Va.

MARSHALL, PETER

(1902-1949). Presbyterian clergyman and chaplain of the U.S. Senate. His posthumous biography, *A Man Called Peter*, written by his wife, gained international acclaim and remained on the best-seller list for some time. Made a Mason in Old Monkland St. James Lodge No. 177, Coatbridge, Scotland. He became a citizen of the U.S. in 1938 and received honorary membership in Temple Noyes Lodge No. 32, D.C. in 1949.

MARSHALL, THURGOOD

(1908-   ). First black U.S. Solicitor General (1965) and first black to be made a Justice of the U.S. Supreme Court (1967) appointed by President Lyndon Johnson. As a lawyer he led the legal battery which won the historic decision from the Supreme Court declaring segregation of public schools unconstitutional (1954). Member of Prince Hall and 33⁰ AASR (PH).

MASARYK, JAN G.

(1886-1948). Vice-Premier and Foreign Minister of Czechoslovakia. His mother was Charlotte Garrigue of Brooklyn, N.Y. and his father the first President of Czechoslovakia. He championed the right of small nations to be free and fought from exile for his country's liberation during WW2. When the Communists took over the government following WW2, he was the last non-Communist in the cabinet. He was found lying in the courtyard of the Czernin Palace on the morning of March 10, 1948. The Communists stated he had committed suicide but it is more probable that he was murdered. Initiated in the Jan Amos Komensky Lodge No. 1 of Prague.

MATHEWSON, CHRISTOPHER "Christy"

(1880-1925). Baseball pitcher for the N.Y. Nat'l League in the early 1900's. His plaque in the Cooperstown Baseball Hall of Fame reads "Matty was Master of Them All." Raised in 1903 at the age of 22 in Architect Lodge No. 519, N.Y.

MAYER, LOUIS B.

(1885-1957). Motion picture producer. His films were among the biggest money-makers in history. Born in Russia and became a citizen of the U.S. in 1912. He received the highest salary in the nation for 7 years (in 1943 it was over a million and a quarter). Many of the top stars were "discovered" by Mayer. Member of St. Cecile Lodge No. 568, N.Y. and a Shriner.

MAYO, CHARLES H.

(1865-1939). Physician who, with his brother William J. (not a Mason) founded the famous Mayo Foundation for Medical Education and Research at Rochester, Minn. in affiliation with the Univ. of Minn. With his brother, donated almost three million dollars for the present Mayo Clinic which began in the Masonic Temple building. Raised in Rochester Lodge No. 21, Minn. in 1890. Also a member of RAM, KT and AASR (SJ). Received the 33⁰ in 1935.

MAYO, CHARLES W.

(1898-1968). Son of Charles H. and surgeon who carried on the work at the Mayo Clinic. Raised in Rochester Lodge No. 21, Minn. in 1920 and member of the RAM, KT. Received the Distinguished Achievement Award of the G.L. of N.Y. in 1958.

MAYO, WILLIAM W.

(1819-1911). Physician and father of Charles H. and grandfather of Charles W. Raised in Rochester Lodge No. 21, Minn. in 1863 in which they also were raised. Member of the RAM and KT.

MAZZINI, GIUSEPPE

(1805-1911). Italian lawyer, patriot and liberator. In 1832 he, with Garibaldi, organized a secret revolutionary society known as "Young Italy" in an effort to unify Italy under a republican form of government. It is not known where he received his degrees, but he was a Mason and Grand Master of the Grand Orient of Italy. The Italian government invited the members of the Grand Orient to participate in the dedication of a statue to Mazzini in Rome in June of 1949 and 3000 Italian Masons were present.

MC ADAM, JOHN L.

(1756-1836). Scottish engineer and inventor of macadamized road building which we have today. He amassed a fortune in the U.S. (1770-83) but returned to Scotland where he died. Master of Lodge Ayr Kilwinning (originally known as Squaremen's) Lodge No. 65, of Ayr.

MELCHIOR, LAURITZ L. H.

(1890-1973). Metropolitan opera tenor who made his debut as a baritone at the Copenhagen Opera in 1913. Also appeared in movies and TV. Raised in St. John's Lodge (Zorobabel og Frederick) No. 1 in Copenhagen; honorary member of Frederick Lodge No. 857, N.Y., 1925. The G.L. of N.Y. gave him the Distinguished Achievement Award in 1944.

MELLON, ANDREW W.

(1855-1937). Industrialist and Secretary of the Treasury, 1921-32. Made a Mason "at sight" by J. Willison Smith, G.M. of the G.L. of Pa. on Dec. 29, 1928 at the same time as his brother Richard B. affiliated with Fellowship Lodge No. 679, Pittsburg. RAM, 1931.

MIX, TOM

(1880-1940). Cowboy, adventurer, soldier, movie actor. Raised in Utopia Lodge No. 537, Calif. in 1925. He was the first of a trio of famous motion picture celebrities to join this lodge, the others being Monte Blue and Richard Arlen. Also member of the RAM and SR (SJ).

MORRIS, ROB

(1818-1888). Masonic lecturer, writer and introduced the degrees which eventually became the Order of the Eastern Star. Raised in Oxford Lodge No. 33, Ky., 1846; Grand Master, 1858. On a trip to the Holy Land he became a charter member of Royal Solomon Mother Lodge No. 293, Jerusalem, which was constituted under the G.L. of Canada, 1873.

MOZART, WOLFGANG AMADEUS

(1756-1791). Austrian composer who created more than 600 works during his life. His greatest work is perhaps *The Magic Flute,* his last opera. Mozart felt that Freemasonry was being persecuted and this opera was intended to vindicate the aims of the Fraternity. He was initiated in Lodge Zur Wohltatigkeit, being No. 20 on the Lodge register. Ten days later (Jan. 7, 1785) he received the second degree in Zur Wahren Eintracht at the request of his mother lodge. His own lodge united with others on Dec. 1, 1785 to become known as Zur Neugekroentin Hoffnung.

NEWTON, JOSEPH FORT

(1880-1950). Clergyman and author who was born in Texas. Raised in Friendship Lodge No. 7, Dixon, Ill. in 1902. Grand Chaplain of the G.L. of Iowa. Author of Freemasonry's classic, *The Builders,* and several other books, Masonic and religious. Received the 33° in 1933.

PEALE, NORMAN VINCENT

(1898-   ). Probably the best known Protestant minister in America (1977). Pastor of Marble Collegiate Reformed Church, N.Y.C. and editor of *Guideposts,* an inspirational magazine. His book, *The Power of Positive Thinking* has gone into many printings. Member of Midwood Lodge No. 1062, N.Y. and Grand Chaplain of the G.L., 1949-51. Received the 33° on Sept. 23, 1959. Shriner.

PEARY, ADMIRAL ROBERT E.

(1856-1920). On his 6th trip, discovered the North Pole on April 6, 1909. Presented a meteorite weighing 90 tons, which he discovered in Greenland, to the G.L. of N.Y. Raised in Kane Lodge No. 454, N.Y., 1896.

PENNEY, JAMES C.

(1876-1971). Founder of the J.C. Penney Co. Lost his fortune in the 1929 crash, but made a brilliant comeback which he attributed to his Christian faith. Known as the "Golden Rule" merchant. Raised in Wasatch Lodge No. 1, Salt Lake City, Ut., 1911. Member of all bodies and awarded the 33⁰ (SJ) on Oct. 16, 1945. Also given the Distinguished Service Award by the Gen. Grand Chapter, RAM in 1958.

PERSHING, GEN. JOHN J.

(1860-1948). Commander-in-Chief of American forces in WW1 and had many honors conferred on him not only by the U.S., but also by other nations. Born in Mo.; graduate of U.S. Military Academy, 1886; LL.B. from Univ. of Neb., 1893. His wife and 3 daughters lost their lives in the burning of The Presidio (Calif.) in 1915. Raised in Lincoln Lodge No. 19, Neb., 1888. Member of both the York and Scottish Rites. 33⁰ awarded in 1930.

PIKE, ALBERT

(1809-1891). Famous Scottish Rite Mason who was born in Boston. When Harvard refused him admittance he went to what was then The Territory of Arkansas. He was a teacher, lawyer and a general in the Confederate Army. Raised in 1850 in Western Star Lodge No. 2, Little Rock. He was never G.M., but was Gr. High Priest of the G.C. RAM of Ark. in 1853-54. His greatest fame was as Grand Commander of the AASR (SJ) from 1859 until his death on April 2, 1891. He did much to revive the Scottish Rite and was compiler of that monumental book, *Morals and Dogma*.

PITTS, WILLIAM S.

(1830-1918). Composer of "The Little Brown Church in the Vale." A music teacher and country doctor. Raised in Bradford Lodge No. 129, Iowa, in the early 60's and became first Master of Mt. Horeb Lodge No. 333, Iowa, 1874; later served as secretary, holding that office until his death.

POLING, DANIEL A.

(1884-1968). Clergyman, lecturer and author. Pastor of the Marble Collegiate Dutch Reformed Church, N.Y.C. from 1922-30. Raised in United States Lodge No. 1118, N.Y and member of the Shrine and AASR (SJ). Given the 33⁰ in 1959.

POUND, ROSCOE

(1870-1964). Former dean of Harvard Law School and probably the greatest authority on Masonic jurisprudence. He served on legal commissions throughout the world. Raised in Lancaster Lodge No. 54, Lincoln, Neb. in 1901 and was Master in 1905. Also a member of Belmont, Beaver and Harvard lodges, all of Mass. Received the 33⁰ in 1913; Gourgas Medal of the SR (NJ), 1940; Dep. G.M. of G.L. of Mass.; holder of Henry Price Medal of Mass. and the Distinguished Service Medal of R.I.

POWELL, JR., ADAM CLAYTON

(1908-1972). Early civil rights leader in the 30's. First black member of U.S. Cabinet (1966). Baptist minister, 1937 until his death. Editor of Negro papers. A Prince Hall Freemason.

PRESTON, WILLIAM

(1742-1818). Much credit goes to him for correcting errors and making the degrees an harmonious unity. His "lectures" formed the basis for much of the present day monitorial work. Born in Edinburgh and made a Mason in 1762 in London. He is best known for his *Illustrations of Masonry*, first published in 1772.

PULASKI, COUNT CASIMIR

(1748-1779). Born in Poland and died in Savannah, Ga. from a wound defending Charleston from the British attack. Benj. Franklin, while in France, met Pulaski and induced him to come to America in 1777. He was introduced to Washington and The Congress "as an officer famous throughout Europe for his bravery and conduct in defense of the liberties of his country against Russia, Austria and Prussia." His lodge is not known but the G.L. of Ga. laid the cornerstone of a monument to his memory in Savannah; Lafayette presided at the ceremonies.

REVERE, PAUL

(1735-1818). Raised in St. Andrew's Lodge of Boston in 1760; G.M., 1795-97. His real name was Paul Rivoire de Romagneu, the son of a French count. We are apt to remember him primarily for the "midnight ride," but he was a celebrated gold and silversmith and his works are prized possessions.

RICKENBACKER, EDWARD V.

(1890-1973). Best known as "Eddie" Rickenbacker. The leading American "ace" in WW1 and in WW2 he made special missions for the Secretary of War to many countries. Forced down on a Pacific flight in 1942 from which he was rescued after three weeks on a life raft. Member of Kilwinning Lodge, No. 297, Mich., 1926; also a member of the other bodies and given the 33° (NJ) in 1942.

RIDGEWAY, GEN. MATTHEW B.

(1895-   ). Chief of Staff, U.S. Army, 1953-55. Raised in West Point Lodge No. 877, N.Y., 1924. Received the 32° (SJ) in Tokyo, Japan, 1951.

RINGLING BROTHERS:

Alfred T. (1861-1919); John Nicholas (?   -1936); Albert Charles (1852-1916); Charles Edward (1866-1926); William Henry Otto (1858-1911); August George (1854-1907); and Henry William George (1868-1918). August Ringling was the father of the 7 brothers. All were raised in Baraboo Lodge No. 34, Wis. The first "wagon show" was in 1884 and this went on to become the "Greatest Show on Earth."

RIZAL, JOSE

(1861-1896). National hero of the Philippines. Made a Mason in Acacia Lodge No. 9, Spain, in 1884; the following year he joined a French lodge in Paris. He is credited with the founding of the lodge "Filipina," and served as Ven. Master of Lakandola Lodge of Perfection, SR. He is known as the "George Washington" of the Philippines.

ROBERTS, ALLEN E.

(1917-   ). Masonic author, speaker, film producer, certified administrative manager, management consultant. His citations and awards are many for his contribution to Masonic education. Four of his documentaries have won Silver Awards and one a Gold Award. Producer of 5 Masonic Leadership Films which are widely used. P.M. of Babcock Lodge No. 322, Va. and Research Lodge No. 1777.

ROGERS, ROY

(1912-   ). Popular radio, movie and TV actor and singer. Raised in Hollywood Lodge No. 355, Calif. Member of SR and Shrine.

ROGERS, WILL

(1879-1935). One of America's best loved humorists and "good will ambassador." His paternal great grandmother was a Cherokee. He made his first appearance on the N.Y. stage in 1905 and joined the Ziegfeld Follies in 1916 where he perfected his monologue technique; appeared in movies and had a syndicated column in many newspapers. Raised in Claremore Lodge No. 53, Okla., 1906. Died in a plane accident in Alaska in 1935 with his friend Wiley Post.

ROMBERG, SIGMUND

(1887-1951). Composer who was born and educated in Hungary. Some of the outstanding hits of the 1900's which he composed were *Maytime, Student Prince, Desert Song, The Night is Young, Rosalie.* Member of Perfect Ashlar Lodge No. 604, N.Y. Made a SR Mason "at sight" on Oct. 25, 1946.

SARNOFF, DAVID

(1891-1971). Called the "father of American television." He came from Russia when only nine. Rose from a messenger to the president of the Radio Corp. of America when 39. Served in WW2 as brigadier general. Raised in Strict Observance Lodge No. 94, N.Y., 1921.

SARTAIN, JOHN

(1808-1897). Engraver who introduced pictorial illustrations in American periodicals. Born in England and came to the U.S. in 1830. The original oil "King Solomon and the Iron Worker," by John Sartain, hangs in the Union Club of N.Y.C. The Macoy Publishing & Masonic Supply Co. obtained reproduction rights from the Sartain estate and prints are to be seen in many lodge halls today. Sartain was a member of Franklin Lodge No. 134, Pa., 1848, and served as Master in 1868; also a member of the KT and given the 33° AASR (NJ).

SCOTT, SIR WALTER

(1771-1832). He was largely responsible for opening the doors in the literary world to another famous Scottish writer and Mason, Robert Burns. Scott was raised in Lodge Saint David No. 36, Edinburgh, in 1801, a lodge in which his father had also been made a Mason.

SIBELIUS, JAN (Jean)

(1865-1957). Finland's greatest composer and the greatest Masonic composer since Mozart. He with others formed Suomi Lodge No. 1 at Helsinki under the G.L. of N.Y. His *Finlandia* and *Masonic Ritual Music* are especially prized by Freemasons and music lovers. Elected Fellow No. 3 in The American Lodge of Research in 1935.

SKELTON, RICHARD BERNARD "Red"

(1910-   ). Comedian who was born in Indiana and started his acting career in a medicine show when 10 years old and from that went to minstrel, show boat, clown in a circus, broadway, radio and movies. Raised in Vincennes Lodge No. 1, Ind. Shriner and given the 33° (NJ) in 1969.

SMITH, SIR C. AUBREY

(1863-1948). Famous English character actor who made many movies in the U.S. Member of Hova Ecclesia Lodge No. 1466, Brighton, England; Master in 1891.

SMITH, DWIGHT L.

(1909-   ). Author of *Whither are We Traveling* (1962) and *Why this Confusion in the Temple?* (1964), two booklets which have met with enthusiastic praise. G.M. of the G.L. of Ind. in 1945-46; editor for several years of the "Indiana Freemason," the official publication of the G.L. For excellence in Freemasonry in general and Masonic writing in particular, he has been honored by the Grand Lodges of Mass., Maine, N.J., Ind. and the Masonic Research Lodge of Conn. Member of Salem Lodge No. 21, Ind. and received the 33⁰ (NJ) in 1949.

SMITH, JAMES FAIRBAIRN

(1902-   ). Born in Scotland and raised as a "Lewis" at the age of 18 in Hawick Lodge No. 111. Editor of the "Detroit Masonic World," but few know that he graduated from the National College of Music (Scotland) and taught music after coming to Detroit for 12 years and was active in founding the Musicians' League, Detroit Conservatory of Music, etc. Member of the RAM and G.H.P. of the G.C. of Mich.; KT, Shriner and member of other bodies. Received the 33⁰ (NJ) in 1934.

SOUSA, JOHN PHILIP

(1854-1932). Member of Hiram Lodge No. 10, D.C., 1881. His father's name was Samuel Ochs. John Philip got the name of "Sousa" from the first letters of *S*amuel *O*chs *U*nited *S*tates *A*merica. This famous bandmaster's most noted work is "The Stars and Stripes Forever." Member of the RAM, KT and Shrine. At the time of his death he had been a Mason more than 50 years.

STANFORD, LELAND

(1824-1893). A lawyer, railroad president, senator and governor who gave 22½ million to establish Leland Stanford Jr. Univ. of Calif. where he is buried. Drove the golden spike at Promontory Point, Utah, May 10, 1869 which joined the Union Pacific and Southern railroads to form the first transcontinental railroad 1776 miles long. Raised in Prometheus (now Ozaukee) Lodge No. 17, Wis., in 1850. When he moved to Calif., he was charter member of Michigan City Lodge No. 47, Calif.

STILLWELL, GEN. JOSEPH W.

(1883-1946). Known as "Vinegar Joe." Served in WW1 and WW2. Raised in West Point Lodge No. 877, N.Y., 1916.

STONE, LEWIS

(1879-1953). Actor who starred in all the "Andy Hardy Family" series. Served in the Spanish-American War and also WW1. Member of Silver Trowel Lodge No. 415, Calif.

STRATTON, CHARLES S.

(1838-1883). Known as "General Tom Thumb" made famous by P. T. Barnum. When Stratton started at a salary of 3 dollars a week and traveling expenses he was about 2 feet tall and weighed 16 pounds. He accumulated a fortune. He married a midget, Lavina Warren, who traveled with him. Raised in St. John's Lodge No. 3, Conn., 1862. Member of all bodies.

SULLIVAN, SIR ARTHUR S.

(1842-1900). English composer who collaborated with W.S. Gilbert in many comic operas, among them *H.M.S. Pinafore, The Pirates of Penzance, The Mikado.* Among his best known songs are *The Lost Chord* and *Onward Christian Soldiers.* His lodge is not known but he was Grand Organist of the G.L. of England in 1887 and a Lodge in Manchester, England, was named for him.

TATSCH, J. HUGO

(1888-1939). Masonic author, banker, curator of the Iowa Masonic Library and G.L. Library of Mass. In WW1 he was a special agent of military intelligence and later became Lt. Col. in the Finance Dept. Vice-President of Macoy Publishing & Masonic Supply Co., Inc., 1927-34. Raised in Oriental Lodge No. 74, Wash., 1909; Master, 1914. Served the Wash. G.L. as Jr. Gr. Deacon and Gr. Orator. Member of many Masonic bodies in U.S. and abroad and died in London, England while delivering a Masonic address at the Authors Club. Received the 33⁰ (SJ) in 1937.

THOMAS, LOWELL

(1892-   ). Known and loved the world over. Author, traveler, lecturer, radio and TV commentator. Historian of note. Raised in St. John's Lodge, Boston, Mass., 1927; dual member of Kane Lodge No. 454, N.Y.

THURSTON, HOWARD

(1869-1936). One of America's greatest magicians. Raised in Manitou Lodge No. 106, N.Y., 1907. Member of the SR and Shrine.

TUBMAN, WILLIAM VACANART SHADRACH

(1895-1971). Black President of Liberia for six terms. Born in London. A Prince Hall Mason and Grand Master.

UPTON, WILLIAM H.

A learned man and a great humanitarian who waged an ardent argument in support of recognition for Prince Hall Masonry while he was Grand Master of the G.L. of Washington (white) in 1898. He published a book, *Negro Masonry; Light on a Dark Subject.*

VINTON, DAVID

(1774-1833?). Wrote the words for Pleyel's Hymn which is still used as a Masonic funeral dirge. The original dirge was first published in 1816 in a volume of Masonic music entitled *The Masonic Minstrel,* which sold more than 12,000 copies. Raised in Mt. Vernon Lodge No. 4, R.I. in 1811.

VOLTAIRE, FRANCOIS MARIE AROUET

(1694-1778). French writer and philosopher. Initiated in Lodge of Nine Sisters, Paris, April 7, 1778 and was escorted into the Lodge by Benjamin Franklin who was then the American Ambassador. Voltaire died shortly after, May 30, 1778.

WAINWRIGHT, GEN. JONATHAN M.

(1883-1953). The hero of Bataan in the Philippine fight for which he was awarded the Congressional Medal of Honor in 1945. Also, served in WW1. Raised in Union Lodge No. 7, Kan., 1946, all in one day, May 16. The next day, May 17th, he received the SR degrees. Also a Shriner.

WALDORF, OSCAR OF THE Real name was Oscar Tschirky.

(1866-1950). Famous Swiss chef who gained fame not only for himself but the Waldorf Hotel in N.Y.C. He probably knew more people from all over the world than any other person in America. Raised in Metropolitan Lodge No. 273, N.Y., 1950.

WALLACE, LEWIS (Lew)

(1827-1905). Lawyer and author of the famous novels, *Ben Hur* and *The Prince of India.* Union Maj. General in the Civil War. Raised in Fountain Lodge No. 60, Ind.

WANAMAKER, JOHN

(1838-1922). Merchant and philanthropist. Established a clothing business in Philadelphia, Pa., in 1861 and one later in N.Y.C. Postmaster General of the U.S. under President Harrison, 1889-93. He gave buildings to the Y.M.C.A., colleges, churches and hospitals not only in the U.S., but also in India, China, Korea and Japan. Made a Mason "at sight" by the G.M. of Pa. on March 30, 1898 and affiliated with Friendship Lodge No. 400, Pa. Served as Master in 1905. Member of the other bodies and given the 33° (NJ) on Sept. 16, 1913.

WARREN, EARL

(1891-1974). Chief Justice of the Supreme Court. Member of Sequoia Lodge No. 349, Calif. Grand Master, 1935-36. Member of the other bodies and received the 33⁰ (SJ) in 1941.

WASHINGTON, BOOKER T.

(1856-1915). Black leader and educator who founded the Tuskegee Institute of Ala. in 1881. Social reformer; author of several books including *Up From Slavery.* Made a Mason "at sight" by the Prince Hall Grand Lodge of Mass.

WATSON, THOMAS J.

(1874-1956). Started his business career with National Cash Register as branch manager and rose to Chairman of the Board of I.B.M. Raised in Valley Lodge No. 109, N.Y., 1901.

WEBB, THOMAS SMITH

(1771-1819). Father of the American ritual first published in 1797, in Albany, N.Y. and entitled *Freemason's Monitor.* Initiated in Rising Sun Lodge No. 39, N.H. Became Master of the G.L. of R.I. in 1813. Dep. Gen. G.H.P., 1816-19. He organized chapters and encampments and the Grand Chapters of Oh. and Ky.

WEEMS, MASON LOCKE

(1760-1825). Author of the fabricated story of Geo. Washington and the cherry tree. An itinerant preacher and bookseller. One of America's first door-to-door salesmen who traveled throughout the South. Member of Lodge No. 50, Dumfries, Va. which became defunct 51 years later.

WESLEY, CHARLES HARRIS

(1891-   ). Black lawyer, professor, university president, Nat. Council YMCA, editor and author of *The History of the Prince Hall Grand Lodge of Ohio, 1849-1870* and *Prince Hall: Life and Legacy,* a dependable look at the man who started black Freemasonry and which dispels legends and presents facts.

WESLEY, SAMUEL

(1766-1837). English composer and organist. He was a nephew of John Wesley (not a Freemason) who founded the Methodist Church. Samuel Wesley built pipe organs and composed a Grand Mass for Pope Pius VI, as well as a set of Matins and Evensongs for the Church of England. Raised in Lodge of Antiquity No. 1, London, 1788. Grand Organist of the G.L. of Moderns and performed at the ceremonies for the United Grand Lodge of England when the two Grand Lodges merged and for which he composed the "Grand Anthem for Freemasons."

WHITEMAN, PAUL

(1890-1967). Known as the "King of Jazz." Traveled extensively throughout the U.S. and Europe with his famous band. Member of St. Cecile Lodge No. 568, N.Y. Member of RAM, KT and Mecca Temple.

WILLIAMS, BERT

(1871-1922). Black comedian and actor who was born in the Bahamas and came to the U.S. as a child. Leading comedian in Ziegfeld Follies. Raised in Waverly Lodge No. 597, Edinburgh, Scotland, 1904. St. Cecile Lodge No. 568 of N.Y. conducted the funeral services in the G.L. Temple, N.Y.C.

WILLIAMSON, HARRY A.

(1875-1965). Black Masonic author who probably did more than any other in his time to raise the standard of Prince Hall Masonry. Raised in Mt. Olive Lodge No. 2, P.H., in N.Y. in 1904. His writings were published in many of the leading Masonic magazines, white and black, in this country, England, Norway, Germany, India, South Africa, Australia and New Zealand. Charter member and second Master of Carthaginian Lodge No. 47. Grand Master of P.H. G.L., 1918-21.

WOOD, GEN. LEONARD C.

(1860-1927). Commander of the "Rough Riders" in the Spanish-American War. Held both medical and law degrees from Harvard. Fort Leonard C. Wood, Mo., is named in his honor. Raised in Anglo Saxon Lodge No. 137, N.Y., 1916. Member of other bodies and elected to receive the $33°$ but died before it could be conferred.

YOUNG, DENTON TRUE "Cy"

(1867-1955). The grand old man of baseball and the first pitcher honored with membership in the Baseball Hall of Fame. He was the only pitcher in the first 100 years of baseball to win 500 games. In all his years he never received more than $2500 a year. Raised in Mystic Tie Lodge No. 194, Ohio, 1904. Also a member of the other bodies and remained an active member until his death.

ZANUCK, DARRYL F.

(1902-   ). Motion picture producer who started out in the advertising field. Member of Mount Olive Lodge No. 506 and Al Malaikah Shrine, Calif.

ZIEGFELD, FLORENZ

(1869-1932). Theatrical producer. Member of Accordia Lodge No. 277, Ill., 1866 and also of the SR (NJ).

ZUKOR, ADOLPH

(1873-1976). Started in the hardware, upholstery and fur business when he came to the U.S. in 1888 from Hungary. Offered American public the first feature-length movie with Sarah Bernhardt in *Queen Elizabeth* (1912) and later built Paramount film empire. Discovered America's sweetheart, Mary Pickford. Member of Centennial Lodge No. 763, N.Y.

PART XVII

Education and Libraries

1. What is the premier Research Lodge of the world?

Quatuor Coronati Lodge No. 2076, London, chartered November 28, 1884.

2. What was the first American Research Lodge?

North Carolina Lodge of Research No. 666, chartered February 10, 1931, Monroe, North Carolina.

3. Are there other English and American Research lodges?

Yes, many. In the United States, the American Lodge of Research in New York is devoted to Revolutionary Masonry. This Lodge was chartered May 7, 1931, in New York City.

4. Where are the five largest Masonic libraries in the United States?

Grand Lodge of Iowa, Cedar Rapids
Grand Lodge of Massachusetts, Boston
Grand Lodge of Pennsylvania, Philadelphia
Grand Lodge of New York, New York City
Supreme Council of the Scottish Rite, Washington, D.C.

5. Is there a national Masonic magazine published in the United States?

No, but several Grand Lodges publish magazines, or bulletins, for their members.

6. Can Masons from other jurisdictions subscribe to these magazines or papers?

Generally, on payment of the subscription rate.

7. Is there a Scottish Rite magazine?

Yes, *The New Age Magazine*, published by the Supreme Council of the Southern Jurisdiction, 1735 Sixteenth Street, N.W., Washington 9, D.C. and *The Northern Light*, P.O.Box 519, Lexington, Mass., the publication of the Northern Jurisdiction.

8. What are some of the Masonic periodicals and where can information as to rates, etc. be obtained?

By writing directly to the magazines, subscription rates or information may be obtained:

Indiana Freemason, Franklin, Indiana
Masonic Messenger, Rome, Georgia
Masonic World, Masonic Temple, Detroit 1, Michigan
The Empire State Mason, New York, N.Y.
The Philalethes, St. Louis, Mo.
The Royal Arch Mason, Trenton, Mo.
Knight Templar, Chicago, Ill.
There are many others.

9. Are there any Negro Masonic magazines?

Yes, the following are the leading ones:
Prince Hall Sentinel, New York, N.Y.
The Light, Pennsylvania
Prince Hall Masonic Review, Georgia
And others.

10. What is perhaps the most widely read Masonic book?

The Builders, by the late Dr. Joseph Fort Newton. No other book has ever taken its place. A new enlarged and revised edition, published in 1951, contains what was probably Dr. Newton's last Masonic writing.

11. What Masonic author and educator has probably done more than any other in modern times to further and encourage Masonic education?

Allen E. Roberts, author of several books including the very popular *The Craft and its Symbols*, written especially for the newly raised Master Mason to answer questions raised in his mind after taking the degrees. Producer of the Masonic Educational Training Program films (5); The Brotherhood of Man Documentary for the M.S.A. His books, *House Undivided* and *Key to Freemasonry's Growth*, have both gone into several printings. His *G. Washington: Master Mason*, published in 1976, has been widely received and enthusiastically reviewed.

12. What recent up-to-date Masonic book will give a comprehensive and authoritative account of history, early and modern, symbolism, customs, etc.?

Coil's Masonic Encyclopedia as well as *Freemasonry Through Six Centuries*, 2 vols. and *Comprehensive View of Freemasonry* by the same author. Also, *Freemason's Guide and Compendium*, by Bernard S. Jones, with a Foreword by J. Heron Lepper, both Englishmen.

13. Who maintains a professorship in George Washington University at Georgetown for special instruction for students wishing to qualify for diplomatic or consular service?

The National League of Masonic Clubs.

14. What is the Masonic Service Association?

A national organization with headquarters at Silver Springs, Md., having an Executive Secretary at the head. It is controlled by all the Grand Lodges who have chosen to become members to promote the very fine educational service which can best be effected through a united organization. The Association is financed on a pro-rata basis by the various Grand Lodges. Educational bulletins are issued and an outstanding service was given during WW2.

15. Do any of the Masonic bodies have "Loan Funds" for educational purposes?

Yes, among them the Supreme Council (Northern Jurisdiction) and the Grand Encampment of Knights Templar for college students.

16. Where can a catalog listing available Masonic books be obtained?

By writing to the publishers of this book. Such catalog lists volumes by many publishers both domestic and foreign, and will be sent without cost.

Macoy Publishing and Masonic Supply Co., Inc.
P.O. Box 9759
Richmond, Va. 23228

PART XVIII

Masonic Regalia

1. Is there a uniform manner of wearing the Masonic apron?

No; even in the E.A., F.C. and M.M. degrees, it varies in the different jurisdictions. In some it is obligatory to wear the apron outside of the garments. Some jurisdictions prescribe an official manner, but the majority do not state how it should be worn.

2: Have Masons always worn a square or "oblong-square" apron?

No. In some jurisdictions, including the United States, some aprons are semi-circular in design. The very early aprons had pockets.

3. Is it permissable to have decorations on Masonic aprons?

Yes, but they are innovations.

4. In New York, nine lodges have special apron borders. What are they?

Lodge No. 2: red; Lodge No. 62: red; Lodge No. 8: orange; Lodge No. 16: yellow; Lodge No. 35: orange; Lodge No. 858: cherry-red and black; Lodge No. 1000: blue on sides and nothing on top and bottom; Lodge No. 1118: blue and gold; American Lodge of Research: light blue.

5. Is there a uniform size for the Masonic apron?

No. The most generally used is 13x15; other sizes are 14x16 and 12x14.

6. Why is Masonic clothing more ancient than the Golden Fleece or Roman Eagle, more honorable than the Star and Garter?

During the Middle Ages those who believed themselves to be "upper-class" looked down on the man who worked. Freemasons then, as now, looked down on a man who did not work, and the Freemason's leather apron became his badge of work.

7. Is it ever proper to wear the Masonic apron in public?

Only for the funeral of a brother, or the performance of some other strictly Masonic duty, such as the laying of a cornerstone.

8. What officer in an English lodge wears a figure of the 47th Problem as his jewel?

The Past Master.

9. How did the Israelites put gold into the garments of the High Priest?

"And they did beat the gold into thin plates, and cut it into wires, to work it in the blue, and in the purple, and in the scarlet, and in the fine linen, with cunning work." *(Exodus 39:3)*

10. Who spoke of the Masonic apron as "the ancient badge wi' the apron strings"?

Robert Burns.

11. What Grand Lodge in the United States has a jewel worn by its Grand Masters which was originally designed for George Washington?

Virginia. The following inscription appears on the reverse side: "Original jewel made in 1778 to be worn by George Washington as first Grand Master of Masons in Virginia. He declined the office, being in command of the Army...."

175

12. In two Grand Jurisdictions of the United States, the Grand Master wears a very large and heavy gold embroidered apron similar to the Grand Master of the United Grand Lodge of England. Which are they?

Massachusetts and New York.

13. "Masonic Clothing" includes what articles?

Apron, collar and jewel, and gloves. In the early day a hat was also part of the "Masonic Clothing" and remains so in a great many American lodges.

14. Modern Freemasons have adopted the apron from the custom of Operative Masons, but were aprons an emblem or symbol prior to Operative Masonry?

Yes, from ancient days the apron has been so considered. It was worn by candidates in many ancient mysteries—Egyptian, Persian, Jewish and Indian. When King Tutankhamen's sarcophagus was opened in 1924, the unwrapping of the mummy of the King revealed an apron, but, as Bernard S. Jones tells us in his informative book, *The Freemasons' Guide and Compendium*, "this gives no ground for presuming that it was a *Masonic* apron."

15. While workmen wore leather aprons for utility reasons, how do we know that not all aprons were of leather?

The word "apron" comes from the French *napron*—meaning cloth. And "a *napron*" has become "an apron."

16. How did we come to trim modern aprons with tassels, rosettes, levels, etc.?

The earliest aprons were plain; strings were placed under the bib or flap, wound around the waist, and were tied in front where the ends hung down, and this in time probably led to the idea of permanent tassels. Rosettes were probably added to indicate rank, two for the Fellowcraft and three for the Master Mason. With the elaborate court costumes, trimmed with lace and braid, it is not difficult to see how Masonic aprons gradually became fancier according to the mode of the day. The side tabs to be found on some of the aprons today are no doubt an outgrowth of the cord and tassels tied in the front. The earliest reference to Masonic levels on aprons appeared in an order of the United Grand Lodge, of England, 1814, when instructions were given for the size and placement.

17. How did we come to wear "Masonic collars"?

The collar has always been a distinguishing mark of office or dignity, and, in addition, it serves a useful purpose for wearing the proper jewel.

18. Why do Masons wear white gloves?

Operative Masons wore gloves to protect their hands, but from Biblical times white gloves have been emblematical of clean hands.

19. Gauntlets are worn by the Grand Officers in some jurisdictions, especially English lodges. From where did this custom come?

In the early Speculative Masonry days, many of the white gloves had gauntlets. As time went on they were ornamented as were the aprons and became so heavy that it was more convenient to have them detached.

20. Why does the Master wear a hat?

The Greeks crowned their warriors with wreaths; caps or halos have long been associated with honor or authority. It has been customary for kings to wear hats in any company, denoting superiority and authority; the Jewish custom of remaining covered in a synagogue is a mark of reverence and respect. From such old traditions it is thought that our Masonic custom derived.

21. In American lodges the emblems for the Deacons are the sun within a sunburst and half moon. What are they for these particular officers in an English lodge?

Dove and an olive branch. In Scotland, a maul and a trowel are used.

22. In English lodges one of the officers wears a jewel depicting a scrip-purse upon which is a heart. What is the name of the officer?

The Almoner.

23. What are commemorative jewels?

Jewels given as a token of appreciation for services rendered such as Past Masters' jewels. They are generally breast jewels, that is, worn on the breast rather than suspended from collars.

24. How should a Masonic ring be worn?

There are no Masonic regulations governing the wearing of personal jewelry or emblems. He who wears a ring for his own enjoyment or as a reminder will wish to wear the ring with the points of the compasses toward his heart. However, emblems are worn for identification purposes and the wearer may wish to wear his ring with the points of the compasses extending outward.

PART XIX

Lodges, Buildings, and Places

1. Where was Fort Hiram?

Providence, Rhode Island, built on October 3, 1814, by 230 Freemasons. It was a breastwork 430 feet long, which was started at 8:00 A.M. and completed by sundown.

2. Who laid the cornerstone of the Statue of Liberty?

William A. Brodie, Grand Master of Masons of New York, on August 5, 1884—"A day of rain."

3. When was the cornerstone of the Washington Monument laid?

On July 4, 1848, with Masonic ceremony.

4. Where is the highest Masonic lodge in the world?

On the crest of Cerro de Pasco, at Oroya, Peru, which is 14,208 feet above sea level. It is Roof of the World Lodge No. 1094, working under the Grand Lodge of Scotland.

5. Where is the highest United States lodge?

At Kokoma, Colorado, which is 10,613 feet above sea level. It is Corinthian Lodge No. 42.

6. Can you name a city in which there is a street or avenue named "Masonic"?

Freemason Street in Norfolk, Va.; Freemason Street in Edenton, N.C.; Freemason Avenue in San Francisco, Calif.; Masonic Lane, Richmond, Va.

7. What Masonic temple is still used in a "ghost" town that was once the capital of the state?

The Masonic Temple at Idaho City, Idaho, where a lodge meeting is held once each year. It stands on perhaps the only piece of ground in the town which has never been mined for gold.

8. There is a Masonic temple in Central America built on piles in a harbor and connected by a bridge to the mainland. Can you name the place or country?

Port Lemon, Costa Rica.

9. There is a lodge in California which opens at midnight once a year. Can you name the lodge and tell why it does this?

Jewel Lodge No. 374, San Francisco, during the Annual Communication of Grand Lodge, for visiting brethren.

10. In the Canal Zone all the land is entirely owned by the United States Government (1978) except one plot. Who owns this?

The Freemasons. A Masonic Temple stands on the land by permission of The Congress.

11. There is a city in Iowa which was originally known as Shibboleth and later as Masonic Grove. Can you give the present name of the city and tell how it got its name?

Mason City, Iowa. This city was founded by a number of Freemasons.

12. There is a city in North Carolina which claims the title, "Most Masonic." What city is it, and why this claim?

Enfield, North Carolina. When this town had a population of 1500 it had a lodge, a chapter, a council, a commandery, a Lodge of Perfection, and a chapter of Rose Croix in the Scottish Rite, and a chapter of the Order of the Eastern Star.

13. On what famous American frigate was a Masonic lodge constituted after the vessel was reconstructed?

"Old Ironsides." Major General Henry Knox Lodge, A.F.& A.M. of Massachusetts was constituted on March 17, 1926, in Charleston Navy Yard at Boston.

14. There are many Masonic lodges in the United States and in other Grand Jurisdictions using the names of Saints. Which are the most popular?

St. Andrew and St. John.

15. There are twenty names of lodges with thirty or more of the same name in the United States and Canada. Which are some of them (excluding Saints as of 1950)?

Star, (197); Light, or Sun, (90); Hiram, (61); Harmony, (60); Washington, (54); Union, (53); Dove, (49); Mt. Moriah, (45); Corinthian, (44); Eureka, (43); Franklin, (42); Unity, (39); Ionic, (39); Solomon, (36); Lafayette, (36); Fidelity, (34); Friendship, (32); Liberty, (30).

16. Where is the Temple of Chichen-Itza?

In a city of that name in Yucatan. It is the remains of a vast ruined pyramid, rich in symbolism.

17. Where is the Temple of Karnak?

At Luxor (Thebes), in upper Egypt. It is constructed with a rare unity of design, testifying to a cooperative system.

18. In English Freemasonry there is a Grand Festival on Saint George's Day. When is it?

April 23rd, to celebrate the Articles of Union uniting the Antients and Moderns.

19. How long have American lodges been celebrating Past Masters Nights?

The first Past Masters Night was held in Asbury Lodge No. 142, F.& A.M., Asbury Park, N.J., on February 22, 1897, and such a night has been held on that date every year since (unless the date falls on Sunday).

20. Name a Masonic body with the Name of a Muse or "Nine Muses."

Loge des Neuf Soeurs, France; Lodge of the Nine Muses No. 235, England; Council of the Nine Muses No. 13, Allied Masonic Degrees, U.S.; Thalia Lodge No. 5177, England.

21. There is a national memorial erected to the memory of George Washington, the Mason. Where is it?

The George Washington Masonic National Memorial is located on Shooter's Hill, in Alexandria, Virginia.

22. When was the movement to erect such a memorial started?

On February 22, 1910, when representatives from eighteen Grand Lodges of the United States met in Alexandria.

23. When was the cornerstone laid?

November 1, 1923, by Charles H. Callahan, of Virginia, who used the same trowel used in laying the cornerstone of the National Capitol by George Washington.

24. When was the memorial dedicated?

On May 12, 1932, again by Past Grand Master Charles H. Callahan, of Virginia.

25. There is a monument to George Washington's mother, Mary, at Fredericksburg, Virginia. What Masonic President laid the cornerstone?

President Andrew Jackson assisted Fredericksburg Lodge No. 4 on May 6, 1833.

26. What Masonic President of the United States was principal speaker at the laying of the cornerstone of the House of Representatives Office Building in Washington?

President Theodore Roosevelt delivered a Masonic address at the occasion on April 14, 1906.

27. The first Masonic lodge in Hawaii was established under what Grand Jurisdiction?

The Grand Orient of France. Two Hawaiian Kings had presided as Masters. The Grand Lodge of California now has lodges in Hawaii.

28. Where did the Temple of Solomon stand?

On Mount Moriah.

29. How long was the Temple of Solomon in building?

7½ years.

30. How long did it stand before being destroyed?

About 435 years.

31. Where is Kilwinning, and for what is it famous Masonically?

The Abbey of Kilwinning is situated in the bailiwick of Cunningham, Scotland. As the city of York, England, claims to be the birthplace of Masonry in England, the village of Kilwinning is entitled to the same honor with respect to the origin of the Order in Scotland.

32. Is there any place where the tide does not ebb and flow twice in twenty-four hours?

Yes, the Gulf of Mexico and the Mediterranean.

33. What lodge has the oldest record in the world?

Edinburgh No. 1, sometimes known as Mary's Chapel No. 1, is believed to be the lodge with the oldest record.

34. What prehistoric temples in America are rich in symbolism?

The Maya and Aztec temples. The rites and ceremonies practiced in them were handed down to the American Indians who practiced a certain form of rites resembling Masonry.

35. Is the old tavern, known as the Goose and Gridiron, in which the first Grand Lodge of England was organized, still standing?

No, it was torn down in 1893-4. It stood near St. Paul's Churchyard, London.

36. Where was Fort Masonic located, and when?

On what was known as the Heights of Brooklyn, New York. It was built by members of fourteen New York Lodges in 1814, agreeable to a resolution of the Grand Lodge, of which DeWitt Clinton was then Grand Master.

37. Are there Masonic lodges in Japan?

Yes, as early as 1866, the G.L. of England had warranted a lodge, followed by others; also, the G.L. of Scotland had warranted lodges, restricted to white members. During WW2, all were suspended and in 1957 the 15 Philippine lodges in Japan formed the G.L. of Japan. Most if not all other G.Ls withdrew their charters. In 1976 there were 21 lodges.

38. What famous church in Paris, in imitation of a Roman basilica, was the work of Operative Masons?

Notre Dame, finished in 1275, by Jean de Chelles, Operative Master Mason.

39. Where is the oldest Masonic Lodge room in the world?

St. John's Chapel, Edinburgh, Scotland (1736).

40. Where is the oldest Masonic Lodge room in the United States?

"Prentiss House," Marblehead, Massachusetts (1760).

41. Where is the oldest Masonic Lodge building?

Lodge Hall of Royal Whitehart Lodge No. 2, Halifax, North Carolina (1771).

PART XX

Oddities

1. What Grand Master in America held the office the longest?

Thomas J. Shryock of Maryland, who held the office for nearly 33 years. He died in office.

2. There were two Grand Masters of England who had thirty-one year terms. Who were they?

The Fourth Duke of Atholl in two different terms, 10 years apart; Augustus Frederick, Duke of Sussex. Two other English Grand Masters served 27 years each.

3. Have there been errors made in Masonic law or official publications which are impossible to effect?

Yes. Once the *Monitor* of one of the United States Grand Lodges had this statement: "Freemasonry unites men of all races, countries, sexes and opinions, provided they become citizens of the United States and residents of the state of...."

4. Have triplets ever been made Masons?

Yes. May 23, 1928, in Madison Lodge No. 93, Madison, N.J., when Alfred, Frederich, and Harold Budd, 23 years of age were raised. Kelsey, Kenneth, and Kermit Grey, also triplets, were Masters of Rising Sun Lodge No. 71, Orland, Maine, in 1935, 1936, and 1937, respectively.

5. What is the largest number of blood brothers being Master Masons?

In 1947, eleven Caldwell brothers made a twelfth brother a Master Mason in Corinthian Lodge No. 96, Barrie, Ontario, Canada. On June 6, 1947, eight Walden brothers made a ninth brother a Master Mason in Twilight Lodge No. 114, Columbia, Missouri. There have been a number of instances of eight and seven blood brothers in one lodge.

6. There are many instances of three blood brothers who have been Masters of a lodge. Are there any records of more than three?

Yes. J.A. Bonner was Master of Eureka Lodge No. 1060, Texas. His six sons were also Masters of this Lodge.

7. What is the largest number of blood brothers made Master Masons at the same time?

The eight Humble brothers, made Master Masons on July 22, 1924, in Brant Lodge No. 45, Brantford, Ontario, Canada; Grand Master W. J. Drope was present for this unusual event.

8. Sons often occupy lodge stations when their father is made a Mason. What is the largest number of sons officiating in such a raising?

Seven. On November 9, 1940, when Joseph Franklin Hughes, 73 years old, was made a Mason in Dangola, Illinois, Lodge No. 581, his seven sons participated.

9. There have been many odd uses of Masonic emblems. What are some of them?

A cattle brand (Square and Compasses) used by Poindexter & Orr Livestock Company, Dillon, Montana, since 1853. Hiram Gasoline Barge, near Highlands, N.J., had square and compasses on its flag. John Wanamaker had square and compasses in the store entrance floor of the large department store in New York City.

10. There have been many unusual lodge meetings. What were some of them?

August 23, 1879, Lodge No. 239, in France, held a meeting in a giant balloon over Paris when a candidate was initiated. August 27, 1919, Oklahoma City Lodge No. 36 started a Communication at noon which did not end until Saturday, August 30th at midnight. Sixty-nine candidates received the Master Mason degree. The Master Mason degree was conferred on a brother 750 feet below ground in the Morton Salt Mine at Grand Saline, Texas, by Grand Saline Lodge No. 1269, in 1940. Sixty took part; it took a half-hour to transport the members to and from the "lodge room."

11. What was the largest Masonic banquet ever held?

At Olympia, England, on August 8, 1925, when 7,000 ate at a celebration of the Festival of the Masonic Million Memorial Fund Drive.

12. Name an unusual Masonic office peculiar to some Grand Jurisdiction?

Grand Clam Baker: California, 1877.

13. What set of Grand Masters are known as the "High Jenks"?

Aldro, Frank, and Maxwell Jenks, who were Grand Masters of the Grand Lodge of Wisconsin in 1896, 1929, and 1937, respectively.

14. A King once acted as Tyler of an American Masonic body. Who was he and over what country was he King?

King Kalakua of Hawaii, when the 29th and 30th degrees of the Scottish Rite were conferred by the Deputy of that district in the King's Palace. Only the King and his brother-in-law had received the degrees, so the King tyled.

15. Tom Thumb has often been referred to as the smallest Mason in the world, but this is not true. Who is the smallest Mason?

Vance Swift, who at 26 years of age, stood 26 inches tall and weighed only 34 pounds when he was made a Mason by Pythagoras Lodge No. 355, New Albany, Indiana, on March 3, 1943. Thumb attained a height of 40 inches and weighed 70 pounds at his death.

16. There is a lodge in New York City which requires brethren who enter or retire to salute the Master and Wardens separately. Which lodge?

Independent Royal Arch Lodge No. 2, F.& A.M.

17. Is it possible for a brother to be Master of two lodges in the United States?

Yes, where dual or plural membership is permitted, but no account of such has been recorded.

18. In what country has this been accomplished several times?

In England. A remarkable case is that of Wor. Brother Victor Dover, Master of Royal Somerset and Inverness Lodge No. 4, the oldest lodge in England, who served simultaneously as Master of Swakely Lodge No. 6634, then the youngest lodge, in 1948.

19. What are the largest number of years recorded as the age of becoming a Mason?

James E. Payne was made a Master Mason in Washington, D.C. at 92 years of age. William G. Hill was made a Mason at 82 years of age in Lodge No. 218, Raleigh, N.C.

20. Is there any instance of a man being a 2½ degree Mason?

Yes. D. Arthur Smally received the first section of the Master Mason degree in Standard Lodge No. 873, Chicago, Ill., at the time of the Iroquois Theater fire. The Lodge went on refreshment and the authorities closed the building. Two weeks later Brother Smally was given the second section of the degree. Another interesting case is that of Lyman C. Van Inwegen, who was called from Mystic Brotherhood Lodge No. 21, Red Bank, N.J., on June 7, 1921, when there was a light failure. Brother Van Inwegen was the superintendent at the electrical plant. He had just received the first section of the Master Mason degree. He did not return that evening and the Lodge was closed. Two weeks later the final section of the degree was conferred on him.

21. Has a man ever received all the Symbolic degrees in one day?

There have been many such instances by the permission of some Grand Master. However, there is one instance which probably will never be duplicated: The Fourth Duke of Atholl (about nine months before he attained his majority) was initiated, passed, and raised, and then installed as Master, and then elected Grand Master—all on the same day, March 1, 1775.

22.   What is the longest proven record of Masonic membership in the world?

Charles McCue, born in McGibbery, Parish of Machremesk County, Antrim, Ireland on June 14, 1756. He was christened in the Church of England by a Rev. Philip Fletcher. According to his G.L. certificate, he was made a Mason in 1775 at 18 years of age (no lodge is given). He came to Canada in 1837 and, on Aug. 7, 1863, affiliated with St. John's Lodge No. 68, Ingersoll, Ont. He died in Ingersoll on May 5, 1870, aged 113 years, 10 months and 9 days. Thus, he was about 95 years a Mason.

23.   What is the longest proven record of Masonic membership in the U.S.?

John Jasper Ray, Sr. who was born on Sept. 2, 1845 in Orange County, N.C. Made a Mason in Gravel Hill Lodge No. 232 in Tenn. March 7, 1868; affiliated with Dublin Lodge No. 504 (Texas). He died in Dublin on May 7, 1952. Thus, he was a Master Mason for 84 years and 62 days.

24.   Have there been many with memberships of 80 years or more?

Only 15 have been recorded (1977).

PART XXI

Miscellaneous

1. How do sizes of Masonic lodges in America differ from the English lodges?

In England there are a great many small "class" lodges, as may be seen by referring to the Grand Lodge of England *Yearbook* which, in 1974, listed 7647 lodges as having been registered. In America the second largest Grand Lodge in the world (New York) shows less than 1000 lodges for the same year.

2. How many white Masons are there in the United States?

According to the Grand Lodge of Iowa Bulletin there were 3,510,225 (1976). The Prince Hall black Masons reported 266,508 members for the same year. No statistics are available for non-Prince Hall black members.

3. How many Masons are there in the world?

Circa 5 million (1976).

4. How many lodges are there in the United States?

15,332 (1976).

5. How many lodges are there in the world?

33,764 (1976).

6. Why is Freemasonry abolished in Fascist, Communistic and Catholic countries?

Because Freemasonry is a democratic organization—primarily Protestant—and all of the above groups are opposed to democratic groups.

7. Can Roman Catholics be Freemasons?

There is nothing in any of the Masonic doctrines, rules, or regulations to prohibit a Roman Catholic from being a Freemason, but the Catholic Church has forbidden (in most countries) its adherents from such membership.

8. How many Presidents of the United States have been Masons?

Fourteen (1976). Washington, Monroe, Jackson, Polk, Buchanan, A. Johnson, Garfield, McKinley, T. Roosevelt, Taft, Harding, F.D. Roosevelt, Truman and Ford.

9. How many Vice-Presidents have been Masons?

Fourteen (1975) proven.

10. In 1943 Hollywood made a Masonic motion picture. What was the name of it?

"Your Son is My Brother."

11. What is an old name for a cornerstone?

A footstone.

12. What Hebrew letter corresponds in force and significance with the Master letter "G"?

The letter jod (Yod), the tenth letter of the Hebrew alphabet, now commonly called *Yodh;* symbol of God.

13. Who said "God perpetually Geometrises"?

Plato.

14. Where do we find the first mention of a secret order by the name of "Eagles" and "Lions"?

In the Mithraic Mysteries.

15. What were the first monuments erected by man?

Altars which were simple squares of rocks "which has not been touched by iron."

16. To what does the term "per capita tax" refer?

To the annual contribution which must be contributed by every member of a given Jurisdiction to Grand Lodge for the expenses of that Grand Body, including various activities conducted by it, such as Masonic Homes, Charity, etc.

17. What great composers have written music especially for Masonic use?

Mozart, Haydn, Liszt, Sibelius, and others. Sibelius, a Fellow of the American Lodge of Research in New York, wrote a series of compositions for use in the "work" of the lodge.

18. What are the three terms used in connection with a candidate receiving the three degrees of the lodge?

Initiated, Passed and Raised.

19. What terms are used for the four degrees of the Chapter?

Advanced, Seated, Acknowledged, and Exalted.

20. In the Council the two degrees have what term?

Greeted.

21. What is the term in the Commandery?

Knighted.

22. What are the two forms of "The Ashlar" used as symbols of Freemasonry?

The Rough Ashlar and the Perfect Ashlar.

23. The meetings of Masonic bodies are designated by different names. What are such names for the Lodge, Chapter, and Council?

Communication, Convocation, and Assembly, respectively.

24. What are the three elements of consecration used Masonically?

Corn, Wine, and Oil.

25. What is the Latin name for the Holy of Holies?

Sanctum Sanctorum.

26. What is wrong with the line "Three or more" used in the opening of a lodge to designate the number necessary to open?

It fails to stipulate that one of the three must be the Master or a Warden.

27. What is wrong with the statement "a certain passage in Scripture which says: 'in strength shall this mine house be established.' "?

There is no such passage in Scripture.

28. Most Grand Lodges have adopted a set of questions and answers for each degree which are used for qualifying purposes. What is the proper name for these?

Catechisms.

29. There have been several court cases based on Masonic fraud. One, however, is outstanding because of its prominence and a book was written covering the case. What was it?

The Thomson Masonic Fraud. The culmination was the conviction, on May 15, 1922, in the Federal Court, at Salt Lake City, Utah, of Matthew McBlain Thomson, Thomas Perrot and Dominic Bergera, of using the mails to defraud. Thomson, the main culprit, served two years in prison.

30. Is the Blue, or Symbolic, Lodge a stepping stone to the so-called "higher degrees"?

No. Masonry does not acknowledge that there are any higher Masonic degrees than the Blue Lodge; the Symbolic degrees are complete. Having received other degrees, a man is no "higher" a Mason than he was after receiving his third degree.

31. Why then is it to a Mason's advantage to take the other degrees?

To add to his knowledge and be better informed on the principles already taught in the Symbolic degrees.

32. In what degree are the true secrets of a Master Mason given?

At no place, nor at any time, are the true secrets of a Master Mason given, for the true secrets are those which the Mason thinks out for himself. They are his personal conceptions and his own conclusions which he has developed from the study of Masonry. And no two will arrive at exactly the same end, for each lives his life as he meets it and not as someone else has tried to have him do. The secrets of a Master Mason represent the individual's incentive to live, to work, and to worship as he chooses and thus make the world a little better for having lived by practicing the moral virtues which Freemasonry has taught him.

33. Is there any special significance to the use of white rods by the Stewards?

This comes from an old English political custom where the Steward of the King's household was appointed by the delivery of a white staff. To dissolve the appointment, the staff was broken.

34. Does Freemasonry recognize any one religion?

No, the Fraternity has never been a part of the Church, or a part of organized religion. Masonic standards are neither for nor against any one creed. Belief in God, the future life, and the brotherhood of man are universal.

35. Is the Great Seal of the United States Masonic?

No, it has no Masonic significance. Although of the three men who were appointed to design the seal, only Benjamin Franklin was a Mason. The Great Seal, adopted in 1782, is indicative of the sense of being in harmony with the eternal wisdom. On the reverse side of the seal is an uncompleted pyramid with an eye surrounded by a Latin motto meaning "God has smiled on our undertakings." Below is another motto meaning "the new order of the ages." (Committee: Adams, Jefferson and Franklin.)

36. When was Masonry first introduced into Norway?

In 1746 when the first lodge was constituted at Christiana (now Oslo) by Count Laurig, in his capacity as provincial Grand Master of the English Grand Lodge.

37. How long does the Grand Master serve in Norway?

He is elected for life.

38. What was the Bull of Pope Clement XII?

An early attack against the Masonic Fraternity in 1738.

39. May a lodge restore a suspended member after his death and give him a Masonic funeral?

No. Such an incident did occur in West Virginia. The Grand Master ruled both the act of restoration and the Masonic funeral illegal.

40. Who wrote the "Enter'd 'Prentice's Song"?

Matthew Birkhead, a member in Lodge V, one of the oldest in London. He was Master of the Lodge before Anderson had published his *Book of Constitutions* in which the song appeared.

41. What was a great undertaking of the Masons in the Province of Alberta?

A "Masonic Farm" of 640 acres was purchased near Lethbridge where youths have a chance for a fair start in the world. Scientific farming is practiced and the principal crops are grain and sugar beets, and live-stock is raised. The purchase is being financed by a contribution from each member of the Fraternity in the Province. In addition to this, a substantial contribution has been made by the Provincial Government.

42. What is wrong in the following Scripture passage as usually recited: "For there the Lord commanded a blessing, even life *forever* more."?

"For there the Lord commanded the blessing, even life for *ever-more.*" (Psalm 133)

43. Where do we find the following line: "The singing Mason building roofs of gold"?

Shakespeare's *Henry V.*

44. Why was the pentagram deemed emblematic of "brotherly love, interlaced, and yet without beginning or end"?

Because the pentagram can be traced by a continuous stroke, returning to the point of beginning, without retracing.

45. Why does the eagle have an emblematical distinction?

Because of the peculiar gift which it possesses of beholding with impunity the undiminished vigor of the sun's meridian rays.

46. Where did Easter get its name?

From Eastre, a goddess for whom a festival was celebrated in April.

47. When was the chisel first introduced into building in England?

William of Sens first introduced it at the re-building of Canterbury Cathedral in 1176. In the preparation of free-stone for building, up to that time, the adze had been used.

48. Who was William of Sens?

The first Master Mason whose works are still extant in England. He was a native of France and is described as *Artifex Subtilissimus*—a most skillful worker.

49. Mention has been made of some famous men as having been made Masons "at sight." What does this mean?

A man is made a Mason "at sight" when any portion of the basic law of a Masonic jurisdiction is set aside by the Grand Master and a degree, or degrees, is conferred on a man who, usually, has not been elected in a lodge. The action itself is based on what has been named "Grand Master's Prerogative." A Mason made "at sight" must be elected in some lodge by affiliation to become a "Mason in good standing."

50. In general, a Grand Lodge cannot confer degrees. In what sort of a Masonic body is a Mason "at sight" made?

In an "Occasional Lodge," the officers of which are selected by the Grand Master. The Grand Master himself is often the Master of such special lodge.

51. Have Masons been made "at sight" in all Grand Jurisdictions in the United States?

No. In some jurisdictions it is specifically prohibited by law. However, even in these jurisdictions it has been done. Such makings are so infrequent that when they are they become "Masonic news."

52. What are some statistics of "at sight" makings in the United States?

In the period from 1875 to 1930, the following cases have been recorded: District of Columbia (3); Indiana (1); Maryland (5); Mississippi (1); Nebraska (2); New Jersey (9); Ohio (2); Oregon (3); Pennsylvania (17); South Carolina (1); South Dakota (1). Out of 45 such makings in the U.S.A. in fifty-five years, 40 were in Pennsylvania.

53. Name some prominent men who were made Masons "at sight."

John Wanamaker (1898); Admiral Winfield Scott Schley (1899); Charles Warren Fairbanks (1904); William Howard Taft (1909); George Wharton Pepper (1925); Andrew Mellon (1928); General Douglas MacArthur (1936); General George Catlett Marshall (1941).

PART XXII

The Eastern Star

1. Where did the Order of the Eastern Star start?

The first organization known as an Eastern Star *Chapter* was formed in New York City, on December 28, 1868, as Alpha Chapter No. 1.

2. Weren't there organizations composed of relatives of Masons before that time?

Yes, several.

3. What were some of these groups called?

Lodges of Adoption; Heroines of Jericho; The Holy Virgin; Masons' Daughter; True Kindred; Good Samaritan; Constellations; Families.

4. Are any of these groups still active?

Yes, the Heroines of Jericho, working the degrees of Master Mason's Daughter, True Kinsman and Heroine of Jericho, is active among the black organizations.

5. There were a number of so-called degrees of the same nature whose rituals were probably never printed, but whose names can be found in the literature of the early 20th Century. What were they called?

Daughters of Bethlehem; Daughters of Zion; Daughters of Zelophadal; Lady of the Cross; Maids of Jerusalem; Sweet Brier.

6. Was the Eastern Star an outgrowth of some of these groups?

No.

7. How was the Eastern Star formed?

Rob Morris of Kentucky received one of the degrees in a group in Mississippi about 1849 and a year later wrote a ritual based on the Eastern Star as a theme.

8. What were the bodies which he formed called?

Constellations.

9. Why did they cease to exist?

They were too elaborate and needed too much dramatic talent for the period.

10. What did Rob Morris do about this?

He reconstructed the degrees in shorter form and formed new bodies called Families.

11. What caused the "Families" to go out of existence?

They did not have enough material in them to hold the interest of the members.

12. What followed then?

Morris turned over his material to Robert Macoy of New York. It was Macoy who reconstructed the material into the degrees of today, known as the Chapter system.

13. What was the first Grand Chapter of the Eastern Star?

New Jersey, July 18, 1870. However, under the rules which governed the individual bodies, it was illegally formed as they did not have "five chapters" which were necessary to the formation of a Grand Chapter.

14. What was the first Grand Chapter organized according to this rule of "five chapters"?

New York, on November 3, 1870.

15. What happened to the New Jersey Grand Chapter?

It was legalized by Robert Macoy in 1873 when they had five chapters.

16. Where and when was the General Grand Chapter of the O.E.S. formed?

At Indianapolis, Indiana, on November 15, 1876.

17. Who was the prime mover of this body?

Rev. Willis Darwin Engle.

18. Do all Grand Chapters now belong to this General Grand Chapter?

No, New York, New Jersey, and Scotland have independent Grand Chapters.

19. Can the members of other Grand Chapters inter-visit with the chapters in New York and New Jersey?

Yes, they all recognize each other.

20. Do Master Masons have to be members of the Order of the Eastern Star in order to visit O.E.S. meetings?

Not in New York and New Jersey; in these two states Master Masons are always welcome.

21. In one state the Eastern Star degrees were given before they were formed into a chapter in New York. In what State?

Michigan.

22. What were these groups called?

Adoptive Lodges, or Lodges of the Adoptive Rite of the Eastern Star.

23. When were they formed?

The first was formed at Rochester, Michigan, on December 15, 1866.

24. What became of this group?

On October 2, 1878, the Grand Body opened its annual session as the "Grand Lodge of Adoptive Rite Masonry," but after its deliberations and resolutions, it closed as the "Grand Chapter, Order of the Eastern Star."

25. Where and when was Rob Morris born?

Born at 26 Rector Street, New York City, on August 31, 1818. He died in La Grange, Kentucky, on July 31, 1888.

26. Where and when was Robert Macoy born?

Born in Armagh, Ulster County, Ireland, on October 4, 1815. He died in New York City, on January 9, 1895.

27. Where and when was Rev. Willis Engle born?

Born in Niles, Michigan, on October 22, 1846. He died in Indianapolis, Indiana, on November 1, 1925.

28. What Grand Lodge forbids Masons to join the Eastern Star?

Pennsylvania.

29. What are the titles of the officers of the General Grand Chapter of the Order of the Eastern Star?

Grand Matron: *Most Worthy;* Grand patron: *Most Worthy;* all others through the Grand Chaplains: *Right Worthy;* for the rest: *Worthy.*

PART XXIII

Androgynous and other Degrees

1. What are androgynous degrees?

Those conferred on both men and women.

2. There are various Orders whose members are composed of relatives of Freemasons. In addition to the Order of the Eastern Star, name others.

The Order of the Amaranth; the White Shrine of Jerusalem; Daughters of the Nile; Order of the Golden Chain; True Kindred of the United States and Canada; Social Order of the Beauceant of the World; Ladies' Oriental Shrine of North America; Daughters of Mokanna.

3. There are groups composed of boys and girls, either sponsored by Masonic or androgynous groups. What are they?

Order of DeMolay for Boys; Order of Rainbow for Girls; Order of Job's Daughters; Daughters of the Eastern Star (Triangle Girls, New York); Constellations (New York).

4. What is the name of the group of Masons composed of men and women?

The Federation of Human Rights, commonly called "Co-Masonry."

5. Where is the headquarters of this group in the United States?

Larkspur, Colorado, six miles from Denver.

6. Is it an American group only?

No; it started in France and spread to England and the United States and now has various bodies in dozens of countries all over the world.

203

7. Is this group recognized by "regular" Masonry?

No, the men who belong have no standing in regular Masonry.

8. Who is probably the most notable woman who was a Co-Mason?

Mrs. Annie Besant, an Englishwoman who, in later years, established headquarters in India.

9. Who founded Co-Masonry in France?

Maria Deraismes, the first initiate, and a Dr. Georges Martin, in 1891.

10. Has there ever been a woman who was a member of a regular lodge?

No. There was never initiated, passed, and raised a woman in a regular lodge, although there are many stories and instances cited. However, investigation of every case known has shown no proof which will stand up under historical research.

11. What are the names of some of the women who were supposed to have been made Masons?

The Honorable Mrs. Richard Aldworth (born the Honorable Miss Elizabeth St. Leger, in 1713). She is supposed to have received the first and second degrees in Lodge 44, Doneraile, Ireland, in 1735. Another is a Mrs. Beaton, in a lodge in Norfolk, County, England, during the 18th Century. A third, Madame de Xaintrailles, of France, who is supposed to have been initiated during the latter part of the 18th Century. A fourth, Mrs. Catherine Sweet Babington, supposed to have been made a Mason in a North Carolina lodge, in 1831.

12. Do the Co-Masons have other forms of Masonry in addition to the lodge?

Yes, they have chapters of Royal Arch Masons, and also confer the Scottish Rite degrees.

13. All Eastern Star rituals today are based on Robert Macoy's *Adoptive Rite Ritual of the Order of the Eastern Star,* **but are there any groups working the true revised Macoy ritual?**

Yes, the black Order of the Eastern Star has a very large and active membership in every state and in foreign countries as well.

14. What is one of the most worthy projects these people have undertaken?

The organization and sponsoring of "Youth Groups."

15. Do the black members of the Order of the Eastern Star have the same aims and purposes in their work as the white members?

Yes, their teachings are the same.

16. What are some of the other groups composed of black members of the O.E.S.?

The Heroines of Jericho; Queen of the South; the Amaranth; Cyrenes; Daughters of Isis; Daughters of Sphinx; The Golden Circle.

17. Do the black Eastern Star members have Grand Chapters?

Yes, but not a General Grand Chapter.

PART XXIV

Masonic Meanings of Words and Phrases

A Masonic abbreviation of a proper word using the first letter such as W∴ for Worshipful; G∴ M∴ for Grand Master, etc.

A. & A.S.R. Ancient and Accepted Scottish Rite (Southern Jurisdiction).

A.A.S.R. Ancient Accepted Scottish Rite (Northern Jurisdiction).

A.A.O.N.M.S. Ancient Arabic Order Nobles Mystic Shrine. "A Mason" can be formed from the first letters of each word.

A.E.O.N.M.S. Ancient Egyptian Order Nobles Mystic Shrine (Prince Hall Shrine).

ABIF. The literal meaning is "his father."

ACCEPTED MASONS. In early days before Speculative Masonry, members who did not necessarily make their livelihood by the building trades, but were accepted into the guilds.

ACCOLADE. Touching the shoulders and head with a sword.

ACKNOWLEDGED. The term used in the Most Excellent Master's degree in R.A. Masonry; when one is initiated he is "received and acknowledged."

ADOPTIVE FREEMASONRY. An organization originally established in France for the initiation of women of Masonic relatives.

ADAM. Derived from the Hebrew *aDaMaH*, meaning "the ground."

ADVANCE. The movement of a candidate who goes from one degree to the next according to his proficiency in the preceding degree.

Ad vitam. Latin for "for life."

A.F. & A.M. Ancient Free and Accepted Masons. There is no particular difference from F. & A.M. (Free and Accepted Masons) or A.F.M. (Ancient Free Masons). Some Grand Lodges use the first designation, others the second. The Grand Lodge of South Carolina uses the last. The difference is traceable to the great schism when there were two Grand Lodges in England–the "Antients" and the "Moderns."

AFFILIATE. From the Latin *filius*, meaning "son." One who has been adopted.

Ahiman Rezon. The name given Dermott's book of constitutions of the "Antients." Interpretations are: "The secrets of a prepared brother" (Dalcho); "the will of selected brethern" (Mackey); "Brother Secretary" (Rockwell).

AHOLIAB. A skillful artificer.

ALCHEMY. Chemistry as practiced during the Middle Ages.

ALLEGORY. Analogy or comparison; a story told to illustrate a principle. It comes from the Greek meaning "to say something different."

ALLOCUTION. An address of the presiding officer.

ALL–SEEING–EYE. An emblem reminding us that we are constantly in God's presence.

"THE ALMOND TREE shall flourish." Signifies old age when the hair turns white.

ALMONER. The dispenser of alms or charity.

ALPHA and OMEGA. First and last Greek letters of the alphabet. The beginning and the end of all things; the first and the last, often mentioned in the Scriptures and in several of the Masonic degrees.

AMARANTH. A plant; the Greek name means "never withering," hence, immortality.

AMBULATORY WARRANT. One which permitted the members of a lodge (usually a military one) to carry the warrant with them and act under it at any place they might be stationed.

AMEN. From the Hebrew meaning "verily, truly, certainly." One person confirms the words of another. Masonically, answered by "So mote it be."

AMERICAN RITE. A name applied to a Masonic system in the U.S. consisting of the Lodge, Chapter, Council, and Commandery.

AMPLE FORM. A Masonic body is opened or closed in "ample form" when the presiding Grand Officer is present. (See "due form")

ANACHRONISMS. Errors as to periods of time or data, used for dramatic or similiar purposes.

ANCHOR AND ARK. That sense of security and stability when our lives are grounded in truth and faith and that without this, there can be no happiness or peace of mind. Hence, emblems of a "well grounded hope and a well-spent life."

ANCIENT CRAFT MASON-RY. The three Symbolic degrees of E.A., F.C., and M.M.

ANCIENT LANDMARKS. Fundamental laws, principles and teachings.

ANCIENT MASONS. See "Antient Masons."

ANCIENT MYSTERIES. Secret societies among the Egyptians, Greeks, and Persians.

ANDROGYNOUS. Derived from two Greek words meaning "a man and a woman." Is applied to those degrees which are conferred on both men and women.

Anno Benefacio. (A.B.) Latin for "In the Year of the Blessing." Used by the Order of High Priesthood for dating their documents. (1930 added to the current date.)

Anno Depositionis. (A.Dep.) Latin for "In the Year of the Deposit."The Cryptic Masonic date designation. (Add 1000 to the current date.)

Anno Domini. (A.D.) Latin for "Year of our Lord."

Anno Inventionis. (A.I.) Latin meaning "In the Year of Dis-

covery." The Royal Arch date designation. (Add 530 to the current date.)

Anno Lucis. (A.L.) Latin meaning "In the Year of Light,"the date used by Ancient Craft Masonry. (Add 4000 to the current date.)

Anno Mundi. (A.M.) Latin meaning "In the Year of the World." The date used by the Scottish Rite. (Add 3760 to the current year until September; if after September, add 3761.

Anno Ordinis. (A.O.) Latin meaning "In the Year of the Order." The date used by the Knights Templar. (Subtract 1118 from the current date.)

ANOINTING. Consecrating a person or thing by the pouring on of oil. Comes from the custom of the Egyptians and Jews.

ANTEDILUVIAN FREEMA-SONRY. One of the traditions that Masonry existed before "the flood."

ANTIENT MASONS, or ANTIENT YORK MASONS. The Grand Lodge established by the Irish Freemasons in England in 1751, distinguished from the first Grand Lodge which the "Antients" termed the "Moderns."

APOCALYPTIC DEGREES. Apocalypsis comes from the Greek meaning "revelation." Those degrees founded on the Revelation of St. John, the Evangelist. (Scottish Rite.)

APPENDANT ORDERS. The degrees of Knight of the Red Cross and Knight of Malta in Templary are conferred as appendages to that of the Order of the Temple which is the principal degree.

APPRENTICE. Comes from the Latin word *apprehendre* meaning "to grasp, to master a thing." Hence, a learner.

APRONS. From the French word *napron* meaning "an apron of cloth." From earliest times in Persia, Egypt, India, the Jewish Essenes, the white apron was a badge of honor and candidates were invested with it, or a sash, or a robe. Its reference is to purity of heart, to innocence of conduct.

ARCANA OF MASONRY. Secrets or mysteries of Masonry.

ARCHETYPE. The original pattern, or mold of a work, or the model from which a thing is formed. In symbolism it is the thing adopted as a symbol.

ARCHIVES OF A LODGE. A place for depositing of records; also, the records themselves.

AROBA, ANCIENT. From the Latin *Arrhabo*, meaning "token or pledge." A pledge or covenant of friendship.

ARREST OF CHARTER. The work of a Lodge is suspended and it is prevented from holding its usual communications by action of the Grand Master. A temporary order until the next meeting of Grand Lodge which is the only body which can approve, revise, or make null the Grand Master's action.

ARYAN RELIGIONS. Include Brahmanism, Buddhism, and the Code Zoroaster.

ASHLAR. A stone as taken from the quarry; an unpolished stone.

ASPIRANT. Comes from the word *aspiro* meaning "to seek eagerly." The Aspirant is one already elected and in process of initiation whereas the Candidate is one who asks for admission.

ASSEMBLY. The meetings of the Council. Also, in the Operative period in the Middle Ages, the meetings of the Craft were called, "assemblies."

ASYLUM. The place of meeting of a Commandery; a place of retreat.

ATHEIST. One who does not believe in God.

ATHOLL FREEMASONS. Sometimes called the "Antient" Freemasons who were presided over by the 3rd and 4th Dukes of Atholl.

Audi, Vidi, Tace. Latin Meaning "Hear, see, and be silent." Found on Masonic medals and documents.

AUM. The Hindu sacred name of God composed of three Sanskrit words. The "A" standing for the Creator; "U" for the Preservor; "M" for the Destroyer or Brahma, Vishnu, and Siva.

A.Y.M. Ancient York Masons (or Masonry)

BADGE OF A FREEMASON. (See aprons)

BALDRIC. A belt worn diagonally across the body from one shoulder over the breast to the hip.

BAPTISM, MASONIC. More properly called "Lustration." Not to be confused with the Christian sacrament. It is a purification by water. Such a ceremony was common to ancient initiations. Clean hands are a symbol of a clean heart.

BATTERY. An acclamation made by clapping the hands in a specific manner for various salutes, especially in connection with the reception of Grand or Supreme officers.

BEAUSEANT. A war banner of the ancient Templars. A black and white banner in the Order of the Temple, the upper black half signifying terror to enemies, the lower white half, fairness to friends.

BEEHIVE. Symbolic of systematized industry. What one may not be able to accomplish alone may be easily performed when all work together at one task.

"BEHOLD YOUR MASTER" and "BEHOLD YOUR BRETHREN." To impress upon the minds of those present of the change of relations and duties assumed.

"BEING A MAN." That he is mature and able to accept the responsibilities of a solemn obligation.

BIBLE BOARD. In Masonic processions, the oldest Master Mason is generally selected as the Bible Bearer to carry the open Bible upon a padded board or cushion. He precedes the Chaplain in procession.

BLAZING STAR. Symbol of light; of Divine direction in the journey through life; symbolizes a true Freemason who, by perfecting himself in the way of truth (knowledge), becomes like a blazing star. In English lodges, symbolizes sun which enlightens the earth, dispensing its blessings to all mankind and giving light and life to all things.

BLUE LODGE. A term which has grown into use over the years meaning the three degrees of the lodge, or Symbolic Masonry. In the early years, Master Masons wore blue lined aprons. Blue is symbolic of perfection, benevolence, truth, universal friendship, fidelity.

BOAZ. Comes from the Hebrew meaning "in strength." The left hand pillar that stood at the porch of King Solomon's Temple.

BOOK OF CONSTITUTIONS. An emblem of law signifying that our moral and spiritual character is grounded in law and order and that no man can live a satisfying life who lives lawlessly.

BOOK OF CONSTITUTIONS GUARDED BY THE TILER'S SWORD. An admonish-ment to the Mason that he should be guarded in his words and actions; obedience to the law.

BOOK OF THE LAW. The sacred book which reveals the will of God. To Christians, the Bible; to the Brahman, the Vedas, etc.

BREASTPLATE. Worn by the High Priest in American R.A. chapters. It is to remind him of his responsibility to the laws of the Order and that the honor and interests of the chapter should always be near his heart.

BRITHERING. The term used for initiation in Scottish lodges.

BROKEN COLUMN. Columns or pillars were used among the early Hebrews to signify nobles or princes; it is from such that we get the expression "pillar of the church." Masonically, the broken column refers to the fall of one of the chief supporters of the Craft.

BURNING BUSH. Fire is a symbol of Deity. The "Bush which was filled with fire and not consumed by it" is the symbol of Divine Light and Truth.

CABALA, or KABBALAH.

211

Mystical philosophy of the Jews.

CABLETOW. The tie by which the candidate is bound to his brethren; the length of a Mason's cabletow is the scope of his ability to go to the relief of a brother in need. In early years the distance was three miles; in present time it is usually considered about forty miles.

CALENDAR, MASONIC. Masons date their official documents in a manner peculiar to themselves. The various dates for the different bodies are based on important points in history. (See *Anno Benefacio*, etc.)

CALLING OFF–CALLING ON. Temporary suspension of labor without the formal closing: "Call from labor to refreshment." Resumption of work is calling on.

CANDELABRUM. Branched candlestick.

CANDIDATE. From the Latin *candidatus* meaning "one who is clothed in white." Candidates for office were clothed in white robes in the early Roman days.

CANDLESTICK, SEVEN BRANCHED. The seven lights represent the seven planets which, regarded as the eyes of God, behold everything. The one in the center signifies the sun or the chief; the other six–three on each side–are the Moon, Mercury, Venus, Mars, Jupiter, and Saturn. The earth was not considered a planet itself, but as receiving light from the seven planets. Uranus was not discovered until 1781 and Pluto not observed until 1930.

CAPITULAR MASONRY. Freemasonry conferred in a Royal Arch chapter in the U.S.

CAPSTONE. The topmost stone in building, the last to be fitted, thus signifying the completed building.

CARDINAL POINTS. East: Wisdom; West: Strength; South: Beauty; North: Darkness.

CARDINAL VIRTUES. Temperance, Fortitude, Prudence, and Justice–the virtues of morality as laid down by Plato. Cardinal comes from the Latin *cardo* meaning "chief or fundamental."

CARPET. A Floor Cloth or mat on which the emblems of a degree are illustrated for instructing candidates. Originally, they were drawn on the floor and then washed off after the lecture. Today, they are commonly called charts and are hung on the wall.

CATECHISM. Instructions of Freemasonry.

CEDARS. Members of the Tall Cedars of Lebanon, a non-Masonic organization composed of Freemasons.

CELESTIAL CANOPY. Symbolic covering of the lodge.

CEMENT. Brotherly love binds Freemasons of all countries, races and creeds in one common brotherhood.

CENSER. Incense urn or cup. A symbol of the pure thoughts and grateful feelings which should be offered up as a fitting sacrifice to God.

CERULEAN BLUE. Sky blue in color.

CHAIN OF UNION. A circle formed by the brethren of a lodge either in a degree or in the opening or closing ceremony.

CHALK, CHARCOAL, AND CLAY. Freedom, fervency, and zeal.

CHARGE. The admonition given at the close of the initiation ceremony to the candidate.

CHARITY, MASONIC. Not only pecuniary help, but "that kindly state of mind which renders a person full of good-will and affectionate regard towards others."

CHARLATAN, MASONIC. One who perverts the Institution of Freemasonry for the acquisition of mere gain, or the gratification of selfish ambition.

CHARTERED LODGE. One which has received authority from the Grand Lodge and is entitled to representation in the G.L.

CHARTER MEMBER. A Freemason who signs a petition as the result of which a Grand Lodge has issued a Charter to a Masonic body.

CHECKERED FLOOR. The Mosaic Pavement.

CHIROMANIA. The peculiar art of speaking with the hands and by gestures, with or without the assistance of the voice.

CHISEL. One of the Working Tools of the Mark Master and symbolizes the advantages of education.

CHIVALRIC MASONRY. Freemasonry conferred in a Commandery, or other Masonic body having Knighthood orders.

CHRISTIAN VIRTUES. Faith, Hope, and Charity.

CIRCLE. A figure which has neither beginning nor end and symbolizes eternity; the universe.

CIRCUMAMBULATION. Comes from the Latin *ambulare* meaning "to walk" and *circum* meaning "around." A procession around the room during certain ceremonies, such as consecration of Masonic bodies, initiation, or advancement of candidates. The Rite of Circumambulation comes from ancient times and refers to the doctrines of sun worship; the procession was made around the sacred place and followed the path of the sun around the earth, from East to South, to West, and back to the East again.

CIRCUMSPECT. A Freemason is charged to be careful in what he says and how he acts that he may not bring dishonor on the Fraternity and himself.

CLANDESTINE MASONIC LODGE. A group of persons uniting into a body termed a Masonic Lodge and purporting to be Masonic, but without the consent of a Grand Lodge. Distinguished from Irregular Lodge.

CLASS LODGES. Those whose members have the same vocation. There are many such lodges in England.

CLEAR OF THE BOOKS. A Freemason who is not in arrears. To apply for a demit, a Mason must be "clear of the books."

CLOTHED, PROPERLY. With white gloves and apron, and the jewel of his Masonic rank. Today the gloves are usually dispensed with.

CODE, THE. Book of Laws of a Grand Lodge (U.S.).

COFFIN. From the Ancient Mysteries, where the candidate was placed in a coffin and then removed, symbolizing a "raising from the dead."

COLLAR. Wearing of the collar and jewel comes from the practices of heraldry. The Masonic collar should be triangular and end in a point on the breast.

COLLATION. A light repast or meal.

COLONIAL LODGES. In America, the early lodges of Colonial times; lodges in the Colonies over which Great Britain ruled are today called Colonial lodges.

COLUMNS. From the Latin *culmen* meaning "a pillar to support or adorn a building." In Masonry the symbolic significance pertains to the supports of a lodge: Wisdom, Strength and Beauty.

COLUMNS, WARDENS. Represent Jachin and Boaz. While the lodge is at work the columns are erect and horizontal, respectively; while on refreshment, such positions are reversed.

CO-MASONRY. A group of Freemasons composed of women and men not recognized by regular Freemasonry.

COMITY. Cooperation, friendliness, courtesy, politeness. Hence, Grand Lodges, while independent, are in external comity with other Grand Lodges which they recognize. Subordinate lodges which cooperate with other lodges, or their own Grand Lodge, are in internal comity with them. All regular lodges and Grand Lodges work together to achieve harmony and peace.

COMMUNICATION OF DEGREES. Bestowed on the candidate by oral description, rather than having the candidate participate. Usually the obligation is given.

COMMUNICATIONS. The meetings of a Symbolic lodge.

COMPASS. A mathematical instrument for dividing and drawing circles; an instrument indicating the magnetic meridian.

COMPASSES. One of the Working Tools. Freemasons have adopted the plural spelling to distinguish it from the magnetic compass.

CONCLAVE. Meeting of the Knights Templar.

CONSISTORY. Meeting of Scottish Rite Masons (19⁰ to 32⁰–N. Juris; 31⁰–32⁰– S. Juris.)

CONTEMPLATIVE FREEMASONRY. Speculative Freemasonry.

CONTUMACY. Refusal to obey an edict of the lodge or Grand Lodge.

CONVOCATIONS. Meetings of the R.A. chapter.

CORNERSTONE. A stone laid at a formal ceremony to celebrate the erection of a public building; a cornerstone joins two walls and forms the foundation of an edifice. In Masonry: a true Mason who has within himself a sure foundation for eternal life.

CORNUCOPIA. The horn of plenty; a symbol of abundance.

CORN, WINE, AND OIL. Three elements of consecration. In ancient times these were regarded as the basic commodities for the support of life and constituted the wealth of the people. Today in the U.S. we think of corn as maize, but the original meaning is an edible grain or cereal. The Hebrew word for corn means "to be increased or to multiply."

COURTESY DEGREES. Degrees conferred by a lodge, or Masonic body, in one jurisdiction for a similar body in another jurisdiction.

COURT OF HONOUR. K.C.C.H. (Knight Commander of the Court of Honour), an honorary degree between the 32⁰ and 33⁰ in the Southern Jurisdiction, A. & A.S.R.

COVENANT. An agreement or contract between two or more.

COWAN. One who may try to pass himself off as a Freemason but who is uninstructed and without "the word."

CRAFT. In Operative Masonry skilled workmen were crafts-men and their organizations were craft guilds. Freemasonry is composed of men skilled in the art of Freemasonry and thus called the Craft.

CREED, MASONIC. A belief in God and in eternal life.

CRESSET. A flaming torch or lamp which is a symbol of light and truth.

CROSIER. The Prelate's staff.

CROW. One of the Working Tools of the Royal Arch. It is an iron implement used to raise heavy objects; symbolically, it is to teach the Companion to raise his thoughts above the world's corrupting influence.

CRYPTIC MASONRY. Freemasonry conferred in the Council of Royal and Select Masters.

"CURIOUS AND CUNNING WORKMAN " Curious comes from the Latin *curiosus* or *cura* meaning "careful." Hence, a careful and skillfull workman.

DAIS. The platform, or raised floor, in the East of the lodge where the Master sits. In the lodge, the steps to this should be three. The Senior Warden's place should be raised two steps and that of the Junior Warden, one step.

DARKNESS. Symbolizes that state of ignorance before light (knowledge) is received.

DEACON. Comes from the Greek *diakonos* meaning "messenger or waiting-man."

DEATH. Symbolical of a completed initiation (work), which has been perfected (entering upon a second Temple), and consumated (finding in the new or second Temple eternal truth).

DECALOGUE. The Ten Commandments.

D.D.G.M. District Deputy Grand Master, an assistant who acts for the Grand Master in a particular district.

"DEDICATED TO THE MEMORY OF THE HOLY SAINTS JOHN." Dedication is a less sacred ceremony than consecration. Hence, lodges are consecrated to God, but dedicated to patrons of the Fraternity.

DEGREE MILL. A body which confers more degrees than is consistent with standard practice.

DEMIT or DIMIT. A release; a resignation of membership; a paper certifying a withdrawal from a lodge (or Masonic body) when in good standing. Both spellings are used, although DIMIT is peculiar to Freemasonry only. In the U.S. some jurisdictions use the former spelling, but the majority use the latter, "Dimit."

DIGEST. Book of laws of a Grand Lodge in the U.S.; sometimes called The Code.

DISPENSATION. Permission to do that which would be forbidden otherwise.

DISTRESS. Physical or mental anguish. A brother in distress does not necessarily mean that he is without funds.

DIVERGENCIES OF THE RITUAL. Each Grand Lodge has its own official ritual which the constituent lodges follow so that every lodge within that jurisdiction will have the same esoteric as well as exoteric or monitorial work. However, there are minor differences in the official rituals of the various Grand Lodges and such are called "divergencies."

Dominus Deus Meus. Latin for "O Lord, my God."

DORMANT LODGES. Lodges which are not active, but which have not surrendered their charters.

DOTAGE. An advanced age when the mind is no longer

able to comprehend clearly.

DOVE. Symbolically denotes peace. In English Freemasonry the Deacons' emblems are the Dove, denoting messengers of the Master and Wardens, in comformity with the doves sent out as messengers by Noah.

DRUID. A Celtic priest.

DUAL MEMBERSHIP. Membership in more than one similar Masonic body, such as in two Symbolic lodges.

DUE. Prescribed action or order.

DUE EAST AND WEST. Moses built the Tabernacle due east and west and this practice was carried on by the church builders. The Freemason travels from the West to the East (light) in search of a Master from whom he may gain instruction, or light.

DUE FORM. A Masonic body is opened or closed in "due form" when performed fully according to a prescribed ritual. Distinguished from "ample form."

DUE GUARD. A mode of recognition peculiar to Freemasons.

DULY AND TRULY PREPARED. That the candidate is truly prepared in his heart and mind to receive further enlightenment; also, properly clothed, Masonically.

EAGLE, DOUBLE HEADED. Is the oldest Royal Crest in the world dating back to the pre-Christian era. The eagle signifies power and domination and when the Roman Empire was divided into the East and the West, a double headed eagle was symbolic of a double empire, and thus displayed in the crest. However, this emblem is known to have been used prior to the Roman Empire era. Masonically, it is the emblem of the Scottish Rite, established no doubt because of the double jurisdiction. The 33⁰ jewel has a golden crown resting upon both heads.

EAR, THE ATTENTIVE OR LISTENING. The Hebrew word means not only to hear, but to understand and to obey.

EAST. From the Sun-worshipers down through the ages, the East has always been considered the most honored place because the sun rises in the East and is the region from which light rises.

EASTER. The first Sunday after

the full moon following the vernal equinox commemorating the resurrection of Jesus Christ. The word comes from the Anglo-Saxon *Eostre* meaning "goddess of spring."

EAVESDROPPER. One who attempts to listen surreptitiously; literally, one standing under the eaves and thus gets only the "droppings."

EBONY BOX. A symbol of the heart used in some of the degrees, intended to teach that in the heart are the secret designs and motives of conduct by which one erects his spiritual temple.

Ecossais. From the French meaning "Scottish."

EDICT. A proclamation or decree issued by a sovereign and having the force of a law.

EDICT OF CYRUS. In 530 B.C. King Cyrus permitted the Jews to return to Jerusalem from Babylonia where they had been held in captivity. They were permitted to rebuild the Temple and their sacred vessels and ornaments of the 1st Temple, which Nebuchadnezzar had confiscated, were also restored to them.

EGYPTIAN FREEMASONRY.

An organization said to have been founded in London in 1776 by Cagliostro. This spurious Rite gained many followers. The late Dr. Henry Ridgely Evans made a lifelong study of this mystery-shrouded adventurer and wrote two books and several articles on the subject.

ELEUSINIAN MYSTERIES. Mysteries of ancient Athenian religion.

EMBLEM. A representation of an idea by a visible object; a symbolical figure or design.

EMBLEMATIC CHART. See Tracing Board.

EMERITUS. From the Latin *emeriti* meaning "to gain by service." In Freemasonry, one who resigns because of age or infirmity, but because of service given, he may be given the title of Secretary Emeritus, etc., though no longer active in the performance of such duties.

EMINENT. From the Latin *eminens* meaning "standing above." Hence, exalted in rank.

ENCAMPMENT. Borrowed from military usage; a temporary gathering of Knights Templar at stated periods.

ENDUE. To invest or clothe

with grace.

ENTERED APPRENTICE. In Operative Masonry the apprenticeship lasted seven years; if then found acceptable, the apprentice's name was entered on the books of the lodge and he was given a recognized place in the craft organization.

EPHOD. Priestly vestment worn by the Jewish High Priest.

ESOTERIC MASONRY. The unwritten work of the ritual which is not to be revealed except to one entitled to receive it.

EVERGREEN. Symbol of immortality of the soul.

EXCULSIVE TERRITORIAL JURISDICTION. The principle that each Grand Lodge is supreme and sovereign within its jurisdiction.

EXEMPLIFICATION OF THE WORK. When the Lecturer performs the ceremonies of a degree for instruction using a Freemason present as substitute for a candidate.

EXOTERIC MASONRY. That which is published, or monitorial work published in the Standard Monitor, and is not secret.

EXPULSION. Forcible ejection from membership for such reasons as un-Masonic conduct, crimes, etc. It is the most severe of Masonic penalties and deprives the person of all rights and privileges formerly enjoyed from his lodge and the Fraternity as a whole.

EXTENT OF THE LODGE. A symbolic expression intended to teach the extensive boundaries of Freemasonry.

EXTERNAL QUALIFICATIONS. Established reputation; social position.

EXTINCT LODGE. One which has ceased to exist and work and whose Charter has been revoked or forfeited.

FAITH. The evidence of things not seen; confidence; trust.

FAITHFUL BREAST. Symbolically, the initiate is instructed that the lessons he has received are to be treasured in his heart and remembered, and not to be forgotten; that which is told in confidence will be so held.

FELLOWCRAFT. A craftsman no longer an apprentice who has been admitted as full member, but who has not yet reached the status of a master. The fellowcraft age represents the stage of manhood.

FEALTY. Loyalty.

Fiat Lux et Lux Fit. Latin motto meaning "Let there be light, and there was light."

FIRST LANDMARKS OF MA-SONRY. Modes of recognition with no variation.

FLAMING SWORD. The flaming sword of the Tiler refers to that which guarded the entrance to Paradise. The blade was a twisted form resembling the ascending flame of fire. Modern Tilers' swords are usually straight.

FLOOR CLOTH. Same as the Carpet, or Floor Cloth on which the emblems of any particular degree are inscribed for use in giving a lecture.

FOOTSTONE. The old name for cornerstone.

FOREIGN COUNTRIES. Higher state of existence after death where the true word, not given in this life, is to be received; where the Master Mason is to enter and then receive wages.

FORM OF A LODGE. An oblong square or parallelogram, twice as long as wide. At the time of the Temple, the only known world was the Mediterranean Sea and the countries to the north, south and east, forming an oblong. Thus, the Freemason's lodge was the world itself.

47TH PROPOSITION OF EUCLID. Derived its name from the fact that it was the 47th problem in Euclid's geometry. Sometimes called problem or theorem, which are also correct. The 47th Proposition, or problem, is to prove that in a right angled triangle, the sum of the squares of the two sides is equal to the square of the hypotenuse. Masonically, it is an emblem of the arts and sciences and reminds us that next to sinfulness, the most dangerous enemy of life is ignorance.

FRATER. Latin meaning *"brother."*

FRATERNAL KISS. A pledge of mutal relief used primarily in Connecticut lodges.

FREE BORN. A free soul; one having attained mastery of himself by self discipline. It is a misconception that this refers to one not born into slavery.

FREEMASONS. The early builders in Operative Masonry times were free men, not serfs or bondsmen and were free to move from

221

one place to another as their work demanded. Thus, they came to be called "Freemasons."

FREE WILL AND ACCORD. That the candidate is capable of choosing right from wrong and deliberately makes the right decision; that a man seeks admisson without coercion or persuasion, but of his own choosing.

FURNIGHINGS OF A LODGE. Holy Bible, Square and Compasses, Charter or Dispensation.

"G". The letter "G" is the Saxon representative of the Hebrew *Yod* and the Greek *Tau*; The initial letter of the name of the Eternal in those languages. It stands not only for God, but for Geometry, that science so important to all Freemasons.

GAVEL. Derives its name from its shape–that of the gable or gavel end of a house. It is a tool used by a stonemason and resembles a hammer having a pointed end for cutting. The Working Tool gavel differs from the upright gavel, or "Hiram." (*See Hiram.*)

GIBBERISH. From the peculiar and mysterious style of writing of Geber, an Arabian alchemist in the 8th century.

GLOBES. Celestial and Terrestrial globes are anachronisms since the world was believed to be flat in ancient days. However, globes, or ovals, have in all ages been symbolic of universality and the Masonic Globes also denote this.

GLOVES, WHITE. Symbolic of purity in the same sense as the white lambskin apron refers to a pure heart, the white gloves refer to clean hands.

GOD. The Hebrew words for Beauty, Strength, and Wisdom (the supports of Freemasonry) are *Gomer, Oz*, and *Dabar*. The initials of these words compose the English name of the Deity.

GOLDEN FLEECE OR ROMAN EAGLE, MORE ANCIENT THAN. The eagle was the Roman symbol of imperial power. The Order of the Golden Fleece was a distinguished Order of Knighthood established in 1429 by the Duke of Burgundy. Fleece was selected as the badge since wool was a staple of the country. It has always been held as one of the most illustrious Orders of Europe.

The Order of the Garter is considered the highest decoration which can be given by the King or Queen of Great Britain.

GRAND EAST. The place where the Grand Lodge holds its communications and from which place the edicts are issued.

GREAT LIGHTS. The Holy Bible, Square and Compasses. The Bible represents the will of God, the Square is the physical life of man and the Compasses represents the moral and spiritual life.

GUILD (GILD) MASONS. Forerunners of the Operative Masons. They were also builders, bound by guild laws and local regulations, but did not have the freedom of moving from city to city.

GUTTURAL. From the Latin *guttur* meaning "the throat."

HEALED. Obligated in a degree which the Mason has not had conferred on him. To "heal" is to "make valid."

HELE. Pronounced "hail" and means to keep guarded, or secret. Sometimes spelled "hale."

HERMES. The Greek God, Mercury.

HERMES TRISMEGISTUS, or The Thrice Great. Sup-posed to have been a great Egyptian philosopher and founder of the art of the Alchemists, or Hermetic science.

HIGH TWELVE. The hour of noon, but Masonically it is the mid-point of the day's work.

HIGHER DEGREES. Additional degrees beyond the first three, or Symbolic degrees. The expression is erroneously interpreted as "superior" degrees. There is nothing "higher" or superior to the Symbolic degrees.

HIRAM. An upright gavel made in the form of a maul and used by a presiding officer.

H.K.T. Hiram, King of Tyre.

HOODWINK. A blindfold which is a symbol of secrecy; mystical darkness.

HOUR GLASS. An emblem of the passage of time.

I.H.S. From the Latin *Iesus Hominum Salvator* meaning "Jesus, Savior of Men."

ILL. Illustrious, a title used in addressing members of the 33⁰.

IMBRUE. To saturate. Often used erroneously for imbue.

IMBUE. To impress, as on the mind; to absorb; tinge deeply.

IMPOSTOR, MASONIC. A man who is not a Mason but seeks to pass himself off as one. An expelled person seeking the privileges of a member in good standing is a Masonic impostor.

INCHOATE LODGE. A lodge working under a Dispensation. The word comes from the Latin *inchoatus* meaning "incomplete."

INEFFABLE. Unutterable.

INHERENT RIGHTS. Immemorial custom, from time immemorial, usually by Royal authority.

In Hoc Signo Vinces. Latin motto meaning "By This Sign Thou Shalt Conquer." The motto used in the Commandery.

INNOVATION. A violation of a Landmark. The word comes from the Latin and means "adding something new."

INNOVATIONS IN MASONRY. The installation charges affirm "it is not in the power of any man or body of men to make innovations in the Body of Masonry." The above charge is only partly used; the original also said, "without the consent of Grand Lodge."

I.N.R.I *Iesus Nazarenus, Rex Iudæorum*, meaning "Jesus of Nazareth, King of the Jews."

IRREGULAR MASONIC LODGE. A Lodge created legally, but continuing to work after its Charter has been revoked. Distinguished from clandestine lodge, and spurious lodge.

I.T.N.O.T.G.A.O.T.U. In the Name of the Grand Architect of the Universe.

JACHIN. Comes from two Hebrew words meaning "God will establish." The right hand pillar of the porch of King Solomon's Temple.

JACOB'S LADDER. Symbol of progress from earth to heaven.

JEWELS, MOVABLE AND IMMOVABLE. The Movable Jewels are the Rough and Perfect Ashlars and the Trestle Board and are so called because they are not confined to any particular part of the lodge whereas the Immovable Jewels: the Square, Level, and Plumb, have definite locations. They are called "jewels" not because of their materials, but because of their meaning. The word "jewel" comes from the Greek meaning "bright or shining."

JEWELS, OFFICIAL. The emblems worn by the officers emblematic of their offices.

J H V H. The Rabinnical perversion is JeHoVaH.

JUST LODGE. One furnished with the three Great Lights. (See "Perfect Lodge" and "Regular Lodge.")

KADOSH. The name of a degree in many Masonic rites.

K.C.C.H. Knight Commander of the Court of Honour, a distinction in the Southern Jurisdiction which precedes the 33º.

KNIFE AND FORK DEGREE. A sarcasm first used by Dermott in his *Ahiman Rezon* denoting Masons who delight in refreshments more than in the labors of the lodge.

KNOCKS. Alarms.

Kodes la Adonai. "Holiness to the Lord," the Royal Arch motto.

Koran, The. The Sacred Volume of Mohammedan Law.

LABYRINTH. A series of intricate winding passages.

LAMB. "In all ages the Lamb has been deemed an emblem of innocence." The candidate is therefore given a white lambskin apron.

LAMB, PASCHAL. The holy lamb offered up by the Jews at the paschal feast, the Passover. It is also a Christian and a Masonic symbol of Christ.

LAMBREQUIN. A drapery hanging from the upper part of a banner.

LANDMARKS. Ancient and universal customs of the Order which gradually grew into operation as rules of action.

LAWFUL AGE. A man of discretion.

LAWFUL INFORMATION. That one has tested by trial and examination, or knows that such has been done by another.

LEGALLY CONSTITUTED. A Lodge working under proper authority and Charter from a Grand Lodge.

LEWIS. An instrument made use of by Operative Masons to lift heavy stones and symbolically, a symbol of strength. More common meaning is the name applied to the son of a Mason who becomes a member of the Craft before he reaches the usual age.

LIBERAL ARTS AND SCIENCES. Grammar, Rhetoric, Logic, Arithmetic,

225

Geometry, Music, and Astronomy.

LIBERTINE. The original theological meaning was one exercising "free thought" or intelligence, but the meaning as used today is very different, "a licentious person."

LILY-WORK. Emblem of peace and unity.

LODGE OF THE HOLY SAINTS JOHN OF JERUSALEM and LODGE OF ST. JOHN. Masonic tradition has it that the primitive, or mother, Lodge was held at Jerusalem and dedicatd to St. John the Baptist, and then to St. John the Evangelist, and finally to both. This Lodge was therefore called "The Lodge of the Holy Saints John of Jerusalem." From this Lodge all other Lodges are supposed, figuratively, to descend.

LOGOS. A Greek word meaning "word or speech."

LOST WORD, SEARCH FOR. That for which the Mason searches is to discover the divine in himself and in the world that he might achieve mental satisfaction and ultimate happiness.

LOW TWELVE. The hour of midnight; darkness is a symbol of death as well as of ignorance.

Lux e tenebris. Latin meaning "Light out of darkness."

MAKING A MASON "AT SIGHT." By a Grand Master's prerogative, some constitutional requirement is set aside–usually the ballot, and a man is made a Master Mason without waiting or instruction between degrees.

MASON. Comes from the Latin *magister* meaning "head" or the French *masoner* meaning "a builder in stone."

MASONIC AGES. The age of an Entered Apprentice is said to be three years (the symbol of peace or perfect harmony); that of a Fellowcraft, five years (the symbol of active life); and that of a Master Mason, seven years (the symbol of perfection).

MASTER'S CARPET. (See "Carpet.")

MASTER'S LODGE. The Ancient Craft lodge. It is the complete and perfect lodge; the Degree of Illumination and Knowledge.

MASTER'S PIECE. Some difficult task of stone cutting or setting.

MORAL LAWS, ESSENTIAL ELEMENTS OF. General

Douglas MacArthur has put it well: "Nothing is to be found in the entire universe which has undergone so little change as the tenets of which moral systems are composed: To do good to others; to forgive enemies; to love neighbors; to restrain passions; to honor parents; to respect authority; to return good for evil; not to cause anger; not to bear false witness; not to lie; not to steal. These are the essential elements of the Moral Law."

MOSAIC PAVEMENT. Tesselated pavement or checkered floor. An inlay floor composed of black and white squares.

MOUTH TO EAR. The method whereby the esoteric work of Freemasonry is passed on from one Mason to another, or from one Mason to the candidate who is qualified to receive such information.

MYSTERIES OF MITHRAS. A part of the Ancient Mysteries, supposed to have been instituted by Zoroaster.

MYSTIC TIE. Spiritual tie not easily broken; fellowship among Masons.

NEITHER NAKED NOR CLOTHED. Neither unclothed, or defenseless, nor clothed and self-sufficient.

Ne plus ultra. Summit of achievement; highest degree.

Ne Varietur. The meaning is "Lest it should be changed." Found on the margin of Masonic certificates where the Mason signs his name; a means of identification.

NOBLES. Members of the Mystic Shrine.

NON-AFFILIATE. A Mason who is a member but not attached to any lodge and temporarily bereft of privilieges. He may be re-affiliated. Distinguished from "Unaffiliated."

NONAGE. Under lawful age.

OATH. A solemn affirmation, in the name of God, that what one testifies is true. Distinguished from:

OBLIGATION. A promise or pledge of obedience. The Mason takes an obligation, not an oath, that he will not depart from the promises he makes.

OBSEQUIES. Funeral rites.

OCCASIONAL LODGE. Similar to a Lodge of Emergency, only one held by a Grand Master for a specific purpose, such as making a Mason "at sight."

OCCULT MASONRY. Masonic philosophies, or degrees, which are more profound than the membership at large comprehends.

OCCULT SCIENCES. Sciences which are hidden from the vulgar; or, in other words, sciences which would not be appreciated or understood by the less educated.

OF GOOD REPORT. That the candidate deserves the good reputation which he enjoys.

OLD CHARGES. Constitutions, rules and regulations of the forerunners of Freemasonry.

ONCE A MASON, ALWAYS A MASON. Even though a Mason is expelled from the Order, his obligation of secrecy is still binding. In this respect only is the phrase a true one for an expelled Mason is no longer entitled to the honors and priviledges of Freemasonry.

OPERATIVE MASONS. Early builders and designers of cathedrals in Europe who were encouraged and sponsored by the Church.

ORIENTAL CHAIR. The seat of the Master in the East; the Oriental Chair of King Solomon.

ORNAMENTS OF A LODGE. The Mosaic Pavement, Indented Tessel, and Blazing Star.

PARALLEL LINES. Lines lying in the same direction, equally distant at all points; symbolic lines of brethren; limits of space.

PARLIAMENTARY LAW, MASONIC. A set of rules adopted by a Grand Lodge, or lodge, in order that its activities may conform to the civil law.

PASSING THE CHAIR. The ceremony of installation of the presiding officer.

PASSWORD. A recognition; a countersign, or intermediate word, between one degree and the next.

PAST RANK. A term attached to granting an honorary title by a Grand Body of Freemasonry. Many distinguished Masons are granted such titles by Masonic bodies out of their jurisdiction. It is also given to brethren in their own jurisdiction, but only rarely in the U.S.

PATENT. A granted privilege evidenced by a letter, certificate, or diploma.

Pax vobiscum. Latin meaning "Peace be with you."

PECTORAL. Pertaining to the breast.

PEDESTALS. The columns

before the Master and Wardens of a lodge.

PENALTIES, MASONIC. Those in the ritual are symbolic only. The only Masonic penalties known to Masonic law are reprimand, suspension, and expulsion.

PENTACLE. A six pointed star formed by two equilateral triangles; also a five pointed star.

PERAMBULATE. To walk over; inspect. Perambulation is the act of passing through; a survey made by traveling.

PER CAPITA TAX. The annual contribution to the Grand Body for the expenses of such body based on the number of members in the subordinate lodge, etc.

PERFECT AHSLAR. Every Mason is expected to perfect or "polish" himself in building his character in order that he may become acceptable in the sight of God and be fit to take his rightful place in the finished work of Masonry.

PERFECT LODGE. One which contains the constitutional number of members.

PERFECT POINTS OF ENTRANCE. Symbolic action called for on entrance into a lodge.

PETITIONER. One who has signed a petition for membership; he remains a petitioner until he has received a favorable ballot. He is then a Candidate until raised.

PHILALETHES. Friends of truth.

PLUMBLINE. The Working Tool of a Past Master; the perfect emblem of uprightness.

PLURAL MEMBERSHIP. Membership in more than two similar bodies, such as in three, or more, Symbolic lodges, Royal Arch chapters, etc.

POMEGRANATE. A fruit symbolic of plenty because of its many seeds.

PONTIFF. A High Priest.

POTENTATE. The presiding officer in a temple of the Mystic Shrine.

POT OF INCENSE. Signifies that, of all forms of worship, it is more acceptable to God to be pure and blameless in our inner lives than anything else.

PROFANE. A non-Mason. The word comes from the Latin *pro* meaning "before" and *fanum* meaning "a temple."

Hence, in Masonry it means those who have not been in the Temple, that is, initiated.

PROFICIENT. Means not only proficient in the ritualistic work, but before the world in daily living.

PROPHETS. Members of the Grotto.

Pro tempore. Latin meaning "for the present time," temporarily.

PUISSANT. Strong; powerful.

PURSUIVANT. Follower; messenger.

REFRESHMENT. Rest period symbolized by noon.

REGULAR LODGE. One working under a charter or warrant from a legal authority.

REPRIMAND. One of the Masonic penalties which can be and is enforced to reprove.

REQUIEM. A hymn for the dead.

RETURNS. Official reports which lodges make to their Grand Lodges.

RITUAL. Comes from the Latin *ritualis* meaning "ceremonial forms."

ROUGH ASHLAR. The unenlightened member; man in his natural state before being educated.

ST. JOHNS' MEN. Those who did not join the Grand Lodge during the first half of the 18th Century. However, they were permitted to visit the regular lodges and signed their names as "St. Johns' Men."

Sanctum Sanctorum. Latin for "Holy of Holies."

SCHISM. A splitting up.

SECRETS, MASONIC. Masonry's only secrets are in its methods of recognition and of symbolic instructions. Its principles and aims have never been secret.

SHASTRAS. The Hindu Sacred Volume of the Law.

SHEKEL. An ancient Jewish coin, or weight.

SHIBBOLETH. An ear of corn; a test word; a watchword; slogan.

SIGNS, MASONIC. Modes of recognition often serving as a reminder of some event or pledge.

SOLSTICE. The point in the ecliptic at which the sun is farthest from the equator (north in summer, south in winter).

SONS OF LIGHT. During the building of King Solomon's Temple the Masons were so called.

SPECULATIVE MASONRY. Freemasonry in its modern acceptance; the application of the implements of Operative masonry to a system of ethics.

Spes mea in Deo est. Latin for "My Hope is in God."

SPRIG OF ACACIA. Symbolizes the immortality of the soul.

SPURIOUS MASONRY. Not genuine; counterfeit; false with knowledge that it is false. Distinguished from *Irregular* Masonry and from *Clandestine* Masonry.

STANDARD WORK. When the work is uniform between the several lodges within a given Grand Jurisdiction.

STARRY-DECKED HEAVEN. Symbolic covering of the lodge.

STATIONS AND PLACES. Officers are *elected* to stations and *appointed* to places.

STEP, THE. Symbolic of the respect and veneration for the altar, whence Masonic light is to emanate.

STRIKING FROM THE ROLL. A punishment inflicted by a subordinate lodge for non-payment of dues.

SUMMONS. A notification from the Master to appear. For its neglect, because it comes directly under the province of his obligation, a member may be disciplined and/or punished.

SUSPENSION. Temporary privation of power or rights, such as suspension for non-payment of dues. One of the Masonic penalties.

SWORD POINTING TO THE NAKED HEART. Signifies that justice is one of the most rigorous laws and if we are unjust in our hearts, the center of our being, the inevitable result of injustice will find us out.

SYMBOL. Signifies or represents some truth, idea or fact, but is not itself the thing it represents.

SYMBOL OF GLORY. The Blazing Star in the old lectures. The star in the center represented Deity, hence, the "Symbol of Glory."

TALMUD. The Jewish civil and canonical laws and traditions.

TEMPORARY LODGES. Those which lasted only so long as a group of Freemasons continued to work together in a given place. There were many of these in Operative masonry.

TENETS OF FREEMASONRY. Dogmas; principles;

teachings of Brotherly Love, Relief and Truth. A Tenet is something obviously true; that which is universally accepted without question.

TESSELATED PAVEMENT. Checkered floor of black and white, symbolic of the triumphs and the despairs throughout life.

TETRAGRAMMATON. A Greek word signifying "four letters." It is a name given by the Talmudists when referring to God or Jehovah.

T.G.A.O.T.U. The Grand Architect of the Universe.

THREE BLOWS. Symbolic of trials to which man is subjected in youth, manhood, and old age; destruction effected by tyranny, superstition and ignorance.

TILER. One who "puts on tiles." The roof of a building is put on last which secures the inner building from outside intrusions. In the early building, tiles were often used as roofing.

TILER'S OATH. An oath taken by a visitor previous to an examination. It was formerly taken in the "Tiler's Room." In some jurisdictions in the U.S. the Tiler's Oath is obligatory; in others it is op-tional and in some it is not used at all.

TILER'S TOAST. A toast to the absent and departed brethren—usually sung by the brethren at nine o'clock.

TOKEN, MASONIC. A sign used for recognition to prove that a man is a Mason.

"TO THAT UNDISCOVERED COUNTRY FROM WHOSE BOURNE NO TRAVELER RETURNS." Comes from Shakespeare's *Hamlet* (Act III, Scene 1).

TRACING BOARD. Or emblematic chart. Emblems used to illustrate the lectures.

TRAVELING FROM WEST TO EAST. In Operative Masonry workmen traveled from one job to another and the word "traveling" came to signify a form of work. Hence, a Mason works his way toward the East (place of light) by improving himself as he progresses through life.

TRESTLE BOARD. The carpet or board upon which the Master inscribes the designs for guidance of the Craft. In the present day it refers to the meeting notice sent to the membership.

TRIALS, MASONIC. Are held in Masonic courts of law in

which testimony is heard and the accused either found innocent or guilty.

TRIUNE. Denoting three in one.

TROWEL. The Working Tool of the Master Mason. Symbolically, to spread the cement of Brotherly Love to fit the capstone to complete the building.

TUBAL CAIN. The first Master Craftsman, son of Lamech and Zillah.

U.D. Under dispensation; a charter not yet having been granted; probationary.

UNAFFILIATED. One who has been expelled, but may be restored to membership. Distinguished from *non-affiliated*.

UNIFORMITY OF THE WORK. (*See* Standard Work.)

UN-MASONIC CONDUCT. Conduct of a Mason which violates the laws of the Craft and his obligation thereto.

UPANISHADS. Vedic literature dealing with the origin of the universe and the coming of man.

USAGE. Mode of using; habitual or long continued use or custom.

VEDAS. One of the four books of the sacred literature of the Hindus.

Veritas. Latin for "truth."

VISITING. Is a privilege and not a right.

V.S.L. Volume of the Sacred Law.

WAGES, A MASTER'S. Symbolizing the fruits of a man's labors in Masonic work.

WARRANT. A commission giving authority.

WINDING STAIRS. Is one which tries a man's soul. He must approach it with faith believing that there is a top, that by a long and arduous climb he will reach a Middle Chamber–a place of light.

"WITHOUT EQUIVOCATION, SECRET EVASION OR MENTAL RESERVATION." The candidate is required to assume obligations with an honest determination to observe them.

WORD, THE. The seeking for truth; experience and accomplishment in living, all directing us to a better life.

WORK, THE. The ritual is called "The Work."

WORKING TOOL OF A PAST MASTER. The plumbline.

WORSHIPFUL. Title of honor

and respect.

WORTHY AND WELL QUALIFIED. That by his character and moral living, the candidate is worthy to be a member.

YEAR, MASONIC. While the civil calendar reckons from the Year of our Lord and is designated A.D., the Masonic calendar dates from the year when God said, "Let there be Light," and is designated A.L.

YOD. (Jod). The tenth letter of the Hebrew alphabet.

YORK RITE. The degrees of the lodge, chapter, council, and commandery.

ZEAL. Intensity of purpose and of earnestness.

ZEND-AVESTA. The Persian Volume of the Sacred Law.

ZENITH. The point in the heavens directly over the head of the spectator; greatest height; symbolically, the plumb, or perpendicular.

PART XXV

MEMBERSHIP STATISTICS IN THE U.S.A. (White)

	M.M.	R.A.M.	R.&S.M.	K.T.
1900	851,970	222,226	46,703	120,763
1910	1,393,894	385,366	104,040	199,250
1920	2,464,330	614,816	213,394	314,588
1930	3,277,513	878,302	311,351	424,981
1940	2,457,263	465,705	153,818	230,989
1950	3,644,634	545,069	174,079	336,329
1960	4,099,219	606,520	190,632	398,564
1970	3,763,213	543,433	207,860	373,815
1975	3,512,628	467,648	216,536	361,525

	32⁰-N	32⁰-S	Shrine	Grotto
1900	25,208	10,570	55,455	1,523
1910	59,301	49,299	149,157	9,207
1920	168,586	161,178	363,744	69,671
1930	286,873	253,898	568,395	145,035
1940	199,743	156,873	316,669	65,038
1950	369,346	353,012	607,915	103,521
1960	481,280	482,927	816,091	82,620
1970	504,308	566,379	870,970	62,700
1975	507,965	613,594	919,032	57,392

	T.Cedars	R.O.S.	Amaranth	*O.E.S.
1900		251		218,240
1910	3,878	419	5,902	533,178
1920	19,386	542	10,932	934,449
1930	41,935	758	45,522	2,171,529
1940	24,472	542	85,217	1,714,127
1950	48,306	879	84,159	2,625,667
1960	53,101	1,437	100,506	2,882,123
1970	41,628	3,283	88,364	2,798,225
1975	36,964	4,448	83,264	2,045,322

*This covers all of the Order of the Eastern Star members in the world. The following figures for 1970 should be subtracted from USA membership in General Grand Chapter as the following four jurisdictions are independent:

New Jersey	54,925
New York	122,724
Canada	86,182
Scotland	400,643
Total	664,474

COUNTRIES	LODGES	MEMBERS
Australia & New Zealand		
New South Wales	886	89,061
New Zealand	433	41,817
Queensland	478	33,655
South Australia	216	20,786
Tasmania	79	8,089
Victoria	829	88,349
Western Australia	305	18,223
7 Provinces	3,226	299,980
Canada		
Alberta (1975)	172	16,145
British Columbia (1975)	170	24,267
Canada (Ontario) (1975)	642	114,749
Manitoba (1976)	106	12,857
New Brunswick (1976)	49	7,797
Nova Scotia (1976)	116	11,358
Prince Edward Island (1976)	17	1,366
Quebec (1976)	108	14,042
Saskatchewan (1976)	182	11,385
9 Provinces	1,560	215,276
Argentina	74	7,000
Austria	33	1,500
China	8	1,220
Costa Rica	10	432
Cuba (1975)	326	25,728
Equador	9	800
England	7,775	600,000
Finland	76	3,100
Germany	372	20,321
Guatemala	26	1,000
India	216	11,000
Iran	38	1,035
Israel	56	3,000
Japan	20	4,495
Netherlands	133	7,100
Norway	27	16,174
Paraguay	5	431
Peru (1974)	118	5,000
Philippines	169	13,198
Puerto Rico	70	5,018
South Africa (1975)	111	4,476
Switzerland	52	3,447
Turkey	53	3,010
23 Grand Lodges	9,777	738,485

COUNTRIES for which no membership statistics are available:

	LODGES
Belgium	32
Chili	135
Colombia	49
Denmark	28
Dominica	22
El Salvador	9
France (G.L.N.)	154
Greece	64
Iceland	8
Ireland	744
Italy	466
Luxembourg	3
Panama	10
Scotland	1,097
Sweden	38
Venezuela	81
16 Grand Lodges	2,940
Mexico: 8 States	375
Brazil: 17 States	554
	3,869

RECAPITULATION OF THE WORLD (1976) STATISTICS
(Based on 1976 *List of Lodges* and the Grand Lodge of Iowa *Bulletin* (1976)

	LODGES		MEMBERSHIP
Grand Lodges U.S.A. (49)	15,332		3,510,225
Other Grand Lodges with known membership	14,563		1,253,741
			4,763,966
Others with no known statistics on membership		at average	
	3,869	of 50 per	193,450
	33,764	lodge	4,957,416

The above covers Grand Lodges listed in the *List of Lodges* but there are others for which no information is available, i.e. Grand Lodge of France, Grand Orient of France, etc. so it can be estimated that the total membership in the world approximates 5 million members.

Also, there are a vast number of lodges and members of black lodges. In 1976 there were 264,312 Prince Hall members in 40 states in addition to 2,196 Prince Hall members in Nassau, Ontario and West Africa.